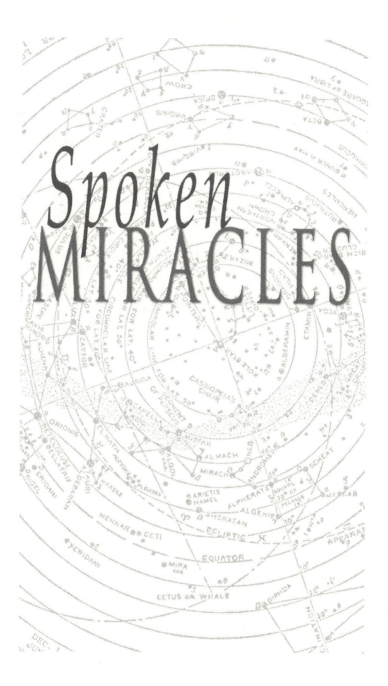

Spoken
MIRACLES

Hay House Titles of Related Interest

Daily Guidance from Your Angels:
365 Angelic Messages to Soothe, Heal, and Open Your Heart,
by Doreen Virtue, Ph.D.

The Disappearance of the Universe:
*Straight Talk about Illusions, Past Lives, Religion, Sex, Politics,
and the Miracles of Forgiveness,* by Gary R. Renard

Enlightenment Cards:
Thoughts from The Disappearance of the Universe,
by Gary R. Renard (a 72-card deck)

The Jesus Code, by John Randolph Price

The Law of Attraction: *The Basics of the Teachings of
Abraham,* by Esther and Jerry Hicks

Secrets of the Lost Mode of Prayer: *The Hidden Power of
Beauty, Blessing, Wisdom, and Hurt,* by Gregg Braden

Your Immortal Reality: *How to Break the Cycle of Birth
and Death,* by Gary R. Renard

ᢟᢟ

All of the above are available at your local bookstore,
or may be ordered by visiting:

Hay House USA: **www.hayhouse.com**®
Hay House Australia: **www.hayhouse.com.au**
Hay House UK: **www.hayhouse.co.uk**
Hay House India: **www.hayhouse.co.in**

Spoken MIRACLES

A Companion to
THE DISAPPEARANCE
OF THE UNIVERSE

Martha Lucía Espinosa

HAY HOUSE, INC.
Carlsbad, California • New York City
London • Sydney • New Delhi

Published in the United States by: Hay House, Inc.: www.hayhouse.
com • **Published in Australia by:** Hay House Australia Pty. Ltd.: www.
hayhouse.com.au • **Published in the United Kingdom by:** Hay House UK,
Ltd.: www.hayhouse.co.uk • **Published in India by:** Hay House Publishers
India: www.hayhouse.co.in

Design: Riann Bender

Library of Congress Cataloging-in-Publication Data

Espinosa, Martha Lucía.
  Spoken miracles : a companion to the Disappearance of the universe /
Martha Lucía Espinosa.
      p. cm.
  Includes bibliographical references.
  ISBN 978-1-4019-1212-3 (tradepaper)
  1. Course in miracles. 2. New Age devotional calendars. I. Renard, Gary
R. Disappearance of the universe. Selections. II. Title.
  BP605.C68E86 2007
  299'.93--dc22

                                                        2006100768

ISBN: 978-1-4019-1212-3

1st edition, July 2007

Printed in the United States of America

To all my children

CONTENTS

FOREWORD

by Gary R. Renard

As the author of the book that this volume is a "companion" to, I was very happy to see Martha Lucía Espinosa become the one to answer a request that has been made by many readers of *The Disappearance of the Universe* (which some of the members of the online discussion group that talks about the book have lovingly referred to as "*D.U.*"). Near the end of *D.U.*, one of my teachers mentioned that there were 365 quotations from the modern spiritual guide *A Course in Miracles (ACIM)* used in the book. We were told that if these passages were read on their own, they could either be used as a thought for the day throughout the year, or they could simply be read like a book, in which case they would constitute a "refresher course" by Jesus, the voice of *A Course in Miracles,* in his own words.

A lot of people requested that this material be compiled into one volume, but it was a bigger job than most realized. My teachers and I had used over 11,000 words from *ACIM* during the course of our discussions. As time went on, it didn't surprise me to see "Lucía," as we know Martha Lucía Espinosa in the online *D.U.* discussion group, step up to the plate and be the one to do the job. She'd become a co-moderator of the electronic forum, and she also had a very busy and successful life and career.

The online discussion group has grown tenfold, reaching over 4,000 members as this book enters its final edition. It's axiomatic that if you want something done, you should ask a busy person to do it. In the last couple of years I've found Lucía to be one of the most dependable people I know, but she's so much more than that. As I learned her story I was amazed by her life experiences, from moving from Colombia to America at the age of 18 to her many extraordinary adventures, which I'll leave for her to tell. In fact, I believe Lucía will be one of the most important teachers of *ACIM* in Spanish, and she has been instrumental in the translation of my first book into that wonderful language, in which *ACIM* is also growing the fastest.

The Disappearance of the Universe isn't a substitute for *A Course in Miracles,* and this book doesn't take the place of *D.U.* I've been told that *ACIM* is like a can, and *D.U.* is like a can opener. It can be very difficult to get into a can without the right tool, but easy when you have it. It can also be tough to understand *ACIM* without the right tool, and *D.U.* has been and will be that tool for many.

This book will add a new dimension to both of the others, for it offers another way of looking at them, which will help illuminate them even more. I'm very grateful to Lucía for putting this work together and making it available to the world. She's earned not only my support but my friendship, too. I wish her success, and I wish you the reader many hours of interesting study while using this fine tool for right-minded thinking. I can't help but believe that this will result in an expanded awareness on the part of any sincere seeker of the truth.

PREFACE

An Essay of Love and Gratitude

In September 2003, I read a book called *The Disappearance of the Universe* by Gary R. Renard (or *D.U.*, as it's known to many of its readers). For the previous three years, I'd also been studying a deeply spiritual work called *A Course in Miracles*, often referred to as *The Course* or *ACIM*. It's a practical spiritual and psychological method for inner transformation that, when put into practice in your life, brings truly miraculous and deeply healing results both within and in your outward life and relationships.

While reading *D.U.*, I realized that my practice and discernment of *ACIM* were being accelerated with the newly gained understanding that the book had brought into my mind after three years of trying to grasp *The Course*'s deeper teachings, which were often interwoven with many everyday practical themes.

The title of this book honors the words originally spoken to the New York–based psychologist who originally took down *ACIM* in shorthand, Dr. Helen Schucman. She transcribed it from a sort of inner dictation that she identified as the voice of Jesus. Over a period of seven years of taking daily dictation (which was typed by her colleague Dr. William Thetford), the process resulted in what eventually became *A Course in Miracles*. Originally published by the Foundation for Inner Peace in 1975, *ACIM* spans over 1,300 pages of Text, a Workbook for Students, and a Manual for Teachers.

Many years after the publication of *The Course,* 365 complete sentences from it were repeated to Gary R. Renard as part of a personalized curriculum from two ascended masters who introduced themselves as two of Jesus's original disciples: Thomas and Thaddeus. The conversations Gary experienced with the ascended masters over a period of nine years resulted in the writing and publication of *The Disappearance of the Universe.*

Gary explains in *D.U.* that over this period of time, his teachers introduced him to *ACIM* and slowly and experientially brought him to a deeper understanding of it. Gary's experience is unique and, of course, initially unbelievable. However, it's trusted by thousands of his readers because of the clarity in its message, which is offered with good humor and exhibits a strong connection with *ACIM.* These factors contribute to the advanced results that both readers of his book and students of *The Course* often experience.

Helen Schucman's experience in transcribing *A Course in Miracles* is also unique and seemingly unbelievable. After all, she said that she received inner dictation for a period of seven years from the voice of Jesus. Yet once a student embarks on a path with this *Course* and deepens the study and practice of what's written in it, the book itself seems to come to life and begin to work with the reader in no less than miraculous ways.

Through the integrated effect of these books in my life, I experienced many miracles. This is why, after reading *D.U.,* I set out to organize all of its quoted material from *ACIM.* I did this both for my benefit and that of other readers who may be as curious as I am to see it all assembled together. And as is mentioned toward the end of *D.U.*, this can be a very helpful "refresher course" on *ACIM*.

After a couple years of research and the generous help that I received in the process, I'm delighted to offer the result. I've received many blessings because of this work, and I know that those who read it will be touched by it as well.

You need not be a Christian to benefit from *ACIM, D.U.*, or this book. The work and teachings reflected in all three stand beyond religious denominations and traditions. In fact, it might be better that you approach all the material with an open mind, thirsty only for truth, hungry only for the love of God or simply something greater in your life—no matter where you may be coming from.

Above all, this book is offered in deep gratitude to Jesus and His ever-present and abundant love in my life.

INTRODUCTION

This book is designed to help those who have read the D.U. book, those who haven't yet, and those who may never do so. Therefore, completing that work isn't a prerequisite for deriving benefit from this one—although judging by the benefits received by thousands of readers of the material, myself included, I do recommend it. This book is also designed to help those who are already students of *ACIM*, those who will study it in the future, and everyone else as well.

Experiences gained through my professional career in information technology and a 30-year spiritual search have taken me down many paths, including various forms of Christianity and much delving into metaphysics, Eastern philosophy, Gnosticism, Hinduism, and alternative theologies. Eventually I found *A Course in Miracles* and the answer to a decades-old prayer. Compiling the quotes from *ACIM* in *D.U.* and finally understanding how God answered my childhood prayers—and everyone else's—has been a blessing.

The title of this book refers to the material in Part II as if it had been spoken, more like *sayings*, although it's actually taken from Gary's first book. I've chosen to do this in reference to the inherent relationship between the *D.U.* words and the Gospel of Thomas, which is a *Sayings Gospel*. This term refers to information recorded by those who actually heard Jesus speak. In contrast with the traditional Gospels, which read more like stories, these works read almost like a transcript or an account of what Jesus might have said. The Gospel of Thomas, discovered in Egypt in 1945 as part of the Nag Hammadi Library, and *D.U.* bear a significant relationship, which I leave to the reader to investigate.

It's also in honor of Thomas and his Gospel that the quotes from *ACIM* are presented in this book as 21st century sayings of Jesus. The material stems from two books in which the scribe and author heard the words as they were spoken to them under miraculous circumstances connected to Jesus.

The book is divided into two parts: Part I tells the story of how the compilation of quotes came about within the context of my experience with *ACIM* and *D.U.,* and Part II contains the material from those books. There are 365 quotes in Part II, which are presented as daily meditations, one for each day of the year. They can also be read straight through as is mentioned in *D.U.* In addition, you can go to either *ACIM* or *D.U.* and study the references within each book's context. Simply follow the references provided.

I hope that you enjoy your journey through these pages.

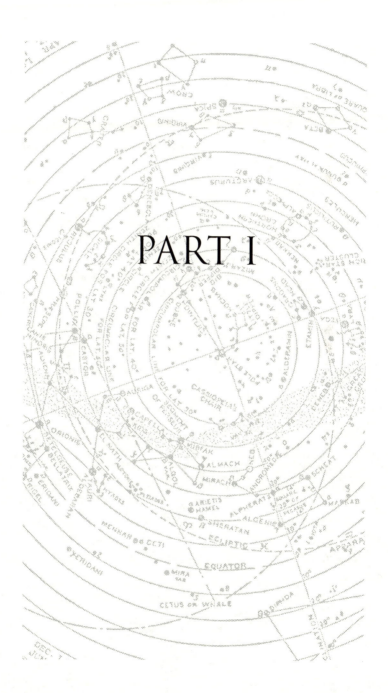

PART I

A Story

*"Let us ask the Father in my name to keep you mindful of His
Love for you and yours for Him. He has never failed to answer
this request, because it asks only for what He has already
willed. Those who call truly are always answered."*
(*ACIM* T-4.III.6:3–5)

Every movie has a hero, and in the movie of your life
you are the hero. What follows is a part of my story. It's
a very small window into a journey that spans over four
decades. I've chosen to share this with you in order to share
the miracle of how these events came to complete a full
circle in the movie of my life.

My hope is that perhaps this little example will help
and motivate you to seek the wonders that are yet to manifest along your path, and that in this, you'll find yourself
one step closer to the perfect joy that God has promised to
all of His children, without exception. For in His perfect
love, which stands forever patient and out of time, no one
is left behind.

CHAPTER 1

Whose Movie Is It, Anyway?

Once upon a time, there was a little girl in a land called Colombia, one of the places known to many as a third-world country. She always wondered what made up the first and second worlds, but never found out. Nor did she discover how that hierarchy was established.

The little girl grew up, eventually emigrated to the United States of America, and seemed to live a hectic life that was sometimes filled with anguish and plenty of stormy nights, as well as countless moments of joy and hope. This was the outer appearance, yet at the same time she had an inner life of constant searching and experimentation in many religions, as well as spiritual and metaphysical paths.

The first conscious step in this search was taken when she was about 13 years old, when a painful experience sent her on a quest to find *her* God. She somehow intuited that the God she'd been told about wasn't the same loving God she knew in her heart.

It was around this time that she went in search of answers and a way to help alleviate the pain that seemed to prevail in the world where she was growing up. She asked God to show her *another way*, because the way in which she was witnessing the world around her did not make sense at all and was in direct conflict with the message of her spiritual teachers at the time.

Among her mentors were the nuns of her Catholic elementary and middle school education; her beloved father, who'd read books by Paramahansa Yogananda and T. Lobsang Rampa to her at bedtime while offering sage advice; her older brother, who'd become her teacher in New Age Gnostic orientation; and the many books she'd read on her own. All of this was quite contrary to the normal education a typical Colombian girl might receive in a society that was 95 percent Catholic, the religion of her mother.

Gnostic philosophy was being taught by a fairly new spiritual group at the time called the Universal Christian Gnostic Movement (UCGM), which presented a different view of New Age Christian thought. It included psychology and spiritual transformation wrapped in Eastern philosophy. It covered subjects such as reincarnation, karma, and ascended masters and the how-to of the processes of ascension, astral projection with purpose, and the like.

UCGM also talked about something that she recognized as uniquely important: the ego, or erroneous concept of the separate "I" self, described as the source of human pain. It taught a method for the dissolution of the ego, and showed how this would lead to an awakening or enlightenment that the girl hardly understood at such an early age. She was young, yet felt so large—as if speeding along a very short runway in order to take off on a long flight. This sensation foretold a lifelong journey.

At an age when most children are still playing ball in the park, this girl spent her days investigating metaphysical writings, taking time to research every new bit of information that came her way. If she'd been able to fast-forward 25 years, she would have seen that she'd eventually come to realize how God always answers everyone, and His reply is always immediate. Yet people sometimes take a while to hear Him, if they do so at all. She'd also come to realize that all her investigations and research were stepping-stones to prepare her to hear the already-given Divine response.

The next few chapters recount the tale of one of those answers. The story is about how God answered the call for help that I made as a child. Perhaps this is your journey, too, but you haven't yet had a chance to hear the Spirit.

In my case, I clamored in anguish for His aid; nearly 25 years later, I heard the reply. At that moment, all sense of time and history were abolished in my mind, and the answer rang true for forever in my heart. After that, I began to listen for the chance to bring my knowledge back to those for whom I'd asked the question in the first place.

Though the events of the following chapters took place in early adolescence, they never faded from my memory. Through the years, they eventually transformed from sad reminiscences into blessed wonders that came to fill my heart with gratitude for God and for the total abundance of His Love. Let's move back in time to hear that first question in order to understand the answer.

CHAPTER 2

The Perennial Question: Why, God?

In about 1975, the girl was about 13 years old and was growing up in the impoverished South American nation of Colombia. During the day, she attended a rigid Catholic school run by Franciscan nuns, while by night she read about gnosis, the psychology of the ego, and anything that was different and could feed her curiosity about the mysteries of life. She learned about paranormal phenomena, reincarnation, UFOs, ancient secrets, sacred texts, and the like.

One day as she was hurriedly walking to the bus stop on her way home from school, she noticed a very old woman walking toward her. The old woman moved slowly and walked with her hands clinging to the building facades that lined the sidewalk, as if either feeling her way along the walls or trying to hold herself up. She took one slow step after another.

The girl couldn't help but fix her gaze upon the old woman. Looking at the lined face, she noticed that the woman wore a grimace of pain, with each step seeming to take a great deal of effort. The girl stopped walking, nearly frozen in place. She finally approached the woman and timidly asked if she was all right and if she needed any help.

In this country, it was commonplace to see street people and beggars, mostly children and the elderly or the insane who roamed the streets in search of scraps of food or a few cents. But this woman's condition was beyond the usual occurrences, and the girl couldn't just walk past her, unimpressed.

The old woman seemed to be near collapse and said that she needed to get home and lie down, but didn't think she could make it. The girl asked what was wrong, and the woman told her how some military policemen had beaten her up with their guns as she'd tried to protect her grandson, who was being falsely accused of subversive activities against the government. He was arrested despite her protests.

The boy was still a teenager and had been taken to an adult prison where he was severely beaten by other inmates and some of the guards. The woman had gone to the precinct where her grandson was being held and tried to reason with the arresting officers to get him released. Her hope never materialized. They'd beaten her up again instead, not listening to any of her pleas.

This story felt totally out of sync with the young girl's reality. She couldn't comprehend this level of abuse and cruelty against an elderly, defenseless woman, and a helpless—and presumably innocent—boy. The girl couldn't make any sense of it and would have preferred to deny that it was real, walking away and forgetting that the encounter had ever happened. She couldn't understand how the God of mercy that she was being taught about could allow such an injustice.

Her mind traveled back over her short life; and she recalled the earthquakes she'd witnessed as an even younger child, the hungry and the poor, and the thousands of homeless children who roamed the streets and slept inside the sewers of the capital, Bogotá. These children, begging outside restaurants where she stopped to eat with her father during trips to the big city, had many times caused her to lose her appetite. She wanted to share her food with them and was unable to swallow when she saw the hunger in their sunken eyes. She'd heard that they sniffed chemicals such as rubber cement and spray paint in order to arrest the hunger pangs in their tummies. There was a deep sense of sorrow, loneliness, and years of neglect that showed through their bony little figures that were in desperate need of washing.

Despite these earlier experiences, this encounter on the sidewalk was the girl's loss of innocence, the moment of her awakening to the reality that betrays childhood bliss. She was making the transition from dreams of play into a new, adult world populated by the nightmares of pain, solitude, and need, which she hadn't truly understood before. She'd been well cared for at home and had never really missed anything, including love and affection from her parents and siblings.

As the girl looked at this poor woman, all kinds of questions swirled around in her mind—questions about the meaning of justice and how it could be exacted in this manner by those who represented her country's government. If they could do this, what then could she expect from the Lord? Yet she *knew* God loved all people. . . . None of it made any sense. This world she was now becoming aware of was sheer madness; something was very much amiss with this new version of "reality."

The girl did the best that a child could do under those circumstances. She hailed a cab, asking the driver for a compassionate discount on his fare in light of the old lady's condition. She also reminded him that she was giving up all of her allowance for the week—she used to save the few pesos her father gave her for snack at recess all week so that she could have a nicer treat on Fridays—which was only enough for half the taxi fare.

The driver was touched by her gesture and agreed to take the old lady home for half the usual charge. The girl helped the old woman get into the vehicle with great difficulty and sent her home, begging the driver to make sure that the grandmother made it into her house safely. He promised that he would, and they parted.

The girl was left sitting on the sidewalk, and she soon began to weep and then sobbed uncontrollably. Her chest ached with a pain that was totally foreign to her. Her throat hurt as she tried to swallow her tears and stop crying, realizing that people who walked by were beginning to notice her distress. Time slipped by as she tried to make sense of Divine justice, human vengeance and cruelty, and her inability to do anything about it. She wanted to understand it all right then and there.

She sat on the side of the street for a long, long time. While her friends were probably at home, playing or doing their homework, there she was, trying to fix the world—and even God. What seemed like hours passed, and she called out to the Lord many times for help and understanding. She felt as though she were screaming at Him from inside her head: *Show me your justice, God! I want to know you. Show your face to me, God! Help me understand. I want to heal their pain! How could you let this happen?!*

As time passed, she grew angrier and more frustrated, feeling impotent at not being able to take the poor woman's pain away and make it all better. What if the lady had died on her way home? Why did it all have to be so ugly? And if she, a mere human child, felt this way, how could God possibly allow such events to occur? It was all beyond her comprehension and terribly painful. She was young, but extremely aware, and she questioned the logic of life. Why did people insist on hurting one another in this way?

She looked around, and for the first time she noticed the impoverished state of her own city's streets: the many potholes, the worried faces, the homeless people, the stray animals and their skeletal figures. She thought about the long walk home that awaited her, which would probably be better than the ride on the decrepit public bus that she could no longer afford after having given her money to the taxi driver. The bus would be crowded with the smell of cigarettes and sweat from all the folks jam-packed in it, one of whom might pick her pockets again, as had occurred the previous week.

As night began to fall, she started to walk. She trudged some 15 blocks while pondering all that had occurred and still asking God for answers. When she arrived home, she was solemn and quiet and opted to go straight to her room. She cried herself to sleep that night, as she did for many nights that followed.

During the days after the incident, she found herself pensive and withdrawn, needing extra energy to return to her normal routine. Eventually she learned to put it all out of her mind and made an effort to return to her busy, studious, lively self. The events of that day began to fade into the forgotten past.

A few months later, she heard of an attraction that had come into town. Her interest in it grew enormously when she found out that it involved demonstrations of paranormal phenomena, one of her key interests. A team of pseudoscientists was staying at the fanciest hotel in town, presenting seminars on hypnosis and experimenting with a new kind of device called a Kirlian camera. This instrument was capable of photographing the human energy field or *aura*.

The girl was beside herself with excitement at the prospect of finding evidence for a fact that she'd intuited: People are more than just bodies of flesh and bone with a silly personality. This thought had occurred to her on many occasions, and now here was proof!

One of her cousins was a local radio personality at the time, and she asked him to give her some time on his show to talk to the Kirlian cameraman on the air. Her cousin agreed, and the man gladly accepted the free publicity. She interviewed him, and it was an experience she never forgot.

This was one of the many things the girl did as an outgoing and precocious child. She wanted to know all about this device and to let everyone else know about it, spreading the word that humans were more than just a physical body. How beautiful everyone is beyond this shell!

She had a picture taken of her thumb's aura, and its beauty mesmerized her. Light rays seemed to emanate from her thumb in hues of white to light yellow and then light blue, to a blue so intense that it looked like the color of a precious gem. The glow finally became a glorious magenta-tinged white, which left her speechless with its beauty.

By the time of the radio interview, the girl had also intensified her studies of Gnostic science. Within weeks of committing to the Universal Christian Gnostic Movement, she'd become an official card-carrying member, and the youngest-ever teacher of metaphysical subjects in her country. By the age of 15, she was studying and teaching seminars on neo-Gnostic principles, which were based on three tenets:

1. Death of the ego self

2. Rebirth of the real self

3. Sacrifice for Humanity—that is, to teach the first through the experience of the second

The workshops also included the study and practice of astral projection, understanding the multiple dimensions of time, lucid-dreaming techniques, meditation, and self-observation. Ultimately, all this led to people awakening to the truth of *being.*

This wasn't enough, however. The girl was too young to really understand the inner workings of human psychology, particularly from within a spiritual context. And as much as she tried to practice everything she knew, she always ended up feeling as though there were something more to learn and that she had a long road to walk in order to fully grasp and then experience it all.

There was also the issue of Jesus. She continually wondered about this mysterious, godlike man who was worshipped by an entire hemisphere. She feared him because her brothers used to scare her with him when they were younger. All the depictions she saw of him in all the churches were based on pain, crucifixion, blood, and death. This fell short of inspiring feelings of love for the image itself, but somehow she felt that the Jesus behind the image was not only important, but crucial to her life and its purpose.

CHAPTER 3

The Answer

Many of us can look back in time and pinpoint a crucial moment in our life, an instant when our entire direction shifted. Had events been otherwise, the unfolding of our journey would have been different altogether.

That fateful day with the old woman developed into the girl's lifelong search for answers to the questions that event elicited, plus all her other queries about Jesus—who he was while he was on Earth some 2,000 years earlier, and why she felt so drawn to him. She also yearned to find others whom she felt were on the same quest and then to share with them. She not only studied gnosis but continued to investigate many sources of esoteric, metaphysical, and psychological learning.

Around the age of 16, she met a man whom she married two years later. He, as an American citizen, was the conduit for her moving to the United States after they wed. She came to his country, grew into womanhood, became a mother, and lived like a regular American citizen herself, yet never did she forget her roots. She was always in search of the answer, which she knew somehow included a different Jesus than the traditional one she also found in this new culture. The American interpretation was a bit kinder, perhaps, yet Jesus was still the same "bookkeeper of sins" from yesteryear and not quite what she was hoping for.

Adventures and misadventures came and went over the next 25 years. During this period, her search never let up. She moved through various spiritual schools of thought, returning eventually to her Christian roots but this time as a born-again Christian. Tears poured down her face on Sunday mornings in church each time she sang, "Open my eyes, Lord. I want to see Jesus, to tell Him I love Him . . ."

She'd continued in her need for answers from God and for more clarity about Jesus himself. She'd accepted him as her savior more than once, but saving her from what? Why did she have to get *saved* every time she met a new spiritual group? What were this "sin" and "hell" that most churches taught? She wanted to see and to know Jesus and his real relationship to God and all of us, and to share with him this *thing* that she felt when she really thought about Him in her heart. But she couldn't describe it in a way that made sense to anyone else.

She yearned to know God and not just know *of* Him. She longed to experience the Divine and often wondered what it would have been like to live 2,000 years ago, when Jesus walked the earth—to hear the sweet word of God's love spring from his sacred holy lips, his love permeating her being in his sweet embrace, his presence real and tangible. What would it be like, to look into his loving eyes? Would she see the infinite?

Her eyes began to tear every time she thought like this. She often asked Jesus why he'd left, why he was here just that once. Why couldn't he come back? She would wash his feet if he did. It would take only one word from him for her to heal—this was her favorite prayer.

After searching and praying for years, she began to think more and more deeply about what it would be like to be with Jesus back then, when he taught his disciples. She read the Bible several times, both in English and Spanish, and began to pray to him directly and to ask for help in hearing him more clearly. She yearned for communion with others who had a different understanding of spiritual matters than what the world presented, and she felt moved to seek more spiritual literature.

Someone at a church had mentioned a book series written by a couple of Christian authors. They were novels that used the story of Revelation as the backdrop for its characters to move through the story of the end of the world, according to their interpretation of this biblical book. She read four of the first five volumes, each of them increasing her unease. In the middle of reading the fifth one, she stopped. A vengeful God, Who would cruelly kill and send His creatures to eternal pain and sorrow in an awful place of His own design, particularly if they happened to be the wrong race and culture (which presumably He had given them), seemed simply irrational.

From where she stood, at age thirtysomething, there was great conflict in traditional Christianity, particularly that which was often called "fundamentalist." There was a sharp contrast between the God of love Who was professed and the God of vengeance Who was hailed and sometimes blamed for all of humanity's woes and made accountable for righteous evils perpetrated by some groups upon others, by many people upon many others.

She found solace and refuge in newer non-Christian, yet deeply spiritual books while keeping up her search. On this new quest, she had increasingly telling experiences that indicated she was approaching something new that was not to be feared, that was completely benign. For example, on a plane ride she was reading a book from a new author who assured readers that he was conversing with God. The passenger next to her noticed the title of the book and asked her what she might be searching for. A perfect stranger was asking her the deepest question of her life!

She replied that she was looking for the truth. He politely asked if he could offer her a gift and gave her an audiocassette. Coincidentally, her hotel room that night just happened to be furnished with a tape player, which never happens. She took this unusual feature to mean she should go ahead and listen to the material, and so she did.

It turned out to be a recording from a retired Catholic priest who was introducing his new series of novels that explored the adventures of a modern-day, wandering Jesus, now called Joshua. What he might be like; how he might talk, dress, act, and relate to others; what he might do to right all the wrongs that everyone is so painfully aware of, yet is accustomed to; and the changes that people experience as he enters a town and stays a little while before moving on to the next one.

She bought and read every one of the books in the Joshua series and sometimes fantasized about meeting the hero herself, all the while still reading the work of the man who was talking with God—the author of the book she'd been reading on the plane.

She decided to attend a seminar led by this "conversations" author in an attempt to learn his technique and to reach out and try to have her very own dialogue with God. Sure enough, in the middle of an exercise at this event, she decided to try and communicate with Him in the form of Jesus. She asked, *Why did you leave us here in this mess and all this suffering? Why did you come here with your message of love just to leave again?*

The answer came undeniably fast, clear, and to the point. Her hand wrote *I NEVER LEFT,* as if by a will that wasn't her own. The words came in all uppercase, which she'd never used as a handwriting style before. She felt in her heart that she'd heard from him, and it seemed as though there was nothing more to write. She waited, but nothing came. That inspired statement was unlike any of her thoughts. It was also quite releasing and imbued with a unique sense of comfort, elicited by the thought itself from within her being. It soothed her immediately, offering her a deep calm and contentment that she'd never felt before.

Sure that she'd heard Jesus reply, she talked to the seminar leader, the well-known author of the conversations books. She told him that as much as she loved his work, she felt that there was no Jesus in his material. She needed Jesus in her life, but not the traditional one of most religions.

The author graciously suggested that perhaps she was ready for a new guide and pointed her toward something called *A Course in Miracles (ACIM),* published by the Foundation for Inner Peace but with no named author. He also recommended other books that had been written about this *Course,* as did other seminar attendees with whom she'd shared her concern.

As if by Divine coincidence, one of the people she met loaned her a book about forgiveness, and it was based on *A Course in Miracles.* She proceeded to read it, and then went through a couple more volumes by other authors who wrote about this subject. The more she read, the more she realized that she needed to go to the source, *The Course* itself, as it's known to its reader-students.

As soon as she returned home from the seminar, she bought *ACIM.* It looked thick, but she was undeterred and began to read in earnest. It contained over 600 pages of Text material, a Workbook for students with 365 lessons for a training program, and a Manual for teachers—more than 1,200 pages. It read quite beautifully, flowed easily, and the more she got into it, the more she noticed that it was mostly written in Shakespearian blank verse, or iambic pentameter. She recognized the style and felt the rhythm in the writing.

It simply filled her with delight. She heard a voice speaking into her heart and mind ever so gently, and slowly walking her through so many points that clarified his being, as well as hers. So crystal clear and so enthralling was the voice that she couldn't stop studying the material for weeks, then months, and finally a few years. Eventually the book itself unveiled what she suspected: This inner speaker not only claimed to be the voice of Jesus, but its loving authority was, in fact, undeniably his.

Studying *The Course* and learning to apply its teaching became her passion. She practiced the lessons in the Workbook and began to experience a world of shifting emotions both within her and in her outer world.

Jesus really lives, she thought, as she realized that she'd found the answer. God is real; God is true. His love *is* perfect. His justice *is* perfect, and so is His creation. We were the ones who chose not to listen to His quiet whisper of love that sings eternally into our deafened ears, forever patient and kind until we choose to listen and return home to Him as prodigal children. He isn't responsible for the world we made. God can't be cruel, for He is perfect Love and fully accessible, no matter what.

It was the answer to the more than 25-year-old prayer she still carried in her heart for the little old lady she'd cared for as a young girl and for all those whom she represented: the poor, the abused, and the neglected. When she'd immigrated to this great new nation of America, she'd found a new kind of society, and her people had become the lowest echelon in it. They were unprotected, underpaid, and overworked, seen as a threat while toiling hard for mere survival. They were the ones on whose behalf she'd been clamoring. She needed to bring the answer back to them to end their suffering. God had made Himself known to her in direct answer to her prayer. She remembered now how she had prayed then: *I want to know You, God, to know Your Justice. The world doesn't make sense. I love you and know that you cherish me, but I need your help in learning to see this.*

This had been her prayer all along. Sometimes it had been silent, and sometimes cried aloud when life got to be just too much to bear.

CHAPTER 4

Clarity

"Miracles fall like drops of healing rain from Heaven on a dry and dusty world, where starved and thirsty creatures come to die. Now they have water. Now the world is green. And everywhere the signs of life spring up, to show that what is born can never die, for what has life has immortality."
(*ACIM* W-340)

ACIM proved to be beautiful, yet challenging to apply and quite deep. I am the little girl in the story, as I mentioned earlier. I studied *The Course* for more than three years and practiced the lessons it prescribed in the Workbook for Students, but I somehow felt that I was progressing slowly.

Even more stormy weather came into my personal life, and the more I studied and practiced, the rougher it seemed to become. You might recall similar moments in your life when you feel as if everything is coming apart, as if there's very little you can do to hold it and yourself together, yet you know you're headed somewhere. You reach out and grasp in the dark for a thread with which to get out of the maze.

This is how I felt throughout 2001 and 2002 as my prayer took on a new form. I asked again for understanding, and for an accelerator of sorts. Somewhere, there was a missing link I wasn't getting in this voluminous material that I knew contained truth. I was failing to fully grasp it.

In August 2003, I attended a seminar in Anaheim, California, that was sponsored by the largest distributor of *ACIM* materials. There, a publisher named D. Patrick Miller was onstage and recommended a book he'd recently put out called *The Disappearance of the Universe.* It had been written by a then-unknown author called Gary R. Renard. I trusted D. Patrick, as I'd also read his balanced journalistic accounts of the history of *ACIM* and other writings. I ordered *The Disappearance of the Universe,* or *D.U.* as its readers now fondly know it, immediately upon returning home from the seminar.

What followed was akin to the experience of intense psychotherapy. It felt as though I were being opened up like a can and poured from the inside out. Many emotions, dreams, visions, ideas, thoughts, feelings, and sensations flowed to finally bring clarity and a sense of true direction and guaranteed peace at the end of this journey. My search came to a stop. Now there was nothing but work left to do in order to reach the goal.

D.U. has been my companion in the study of *A Course in Miracles* ever since, and it proved to be a spiritual accelerator. It also sealed the answer to my childhood prayer about God's impossible cruelty and endless and flawless unconditional love for all of His creations. Most of all, it offered a clearer understanding of a simple process of advanced forgiveness that helped me find the way home again along with all of God's children—not some, but all. There are no exceptions in His infinite mercy and complete, perfect love, which casts out all fear and where no one is left behind—a gospel of complete inclusion and of perfect mercy.

"If God was the maker of this world, He would indeed be a cruel God," says *D.U.* Now, at first glance this statement doesn't sit well with our traditional upbringing. In fact, we may tremble in fear when we read it, seeing it as blasphemy or heresy, based on what we've been taught. Yet this simple misunderstanding is the source of all our pain and the block to accepting God's completely benign presence in our lives. We see Him as the maker of both our joys and our sorrows, and this causes us distress. We then see Him within the frame of a fearful and withdrawn dualistic perspective, where God has two faces, not one, and a flimsy will. As a defense, we set out to make a will that isn't His but ours and are destined to live in endless competition with the Almighty, who does nothing in return but love without end. God is infinite love. And not only is that all that He is, but that's all there is, all that you are, and all that I am.

However, in order to see this truth clearly and experientially, you must purposely and voluntarily take on your cross. You must be willing to give up and remove the blocks to the awareness of love's presence in you. The speck that Jesus spoke about in Matthew 7:5 is in your own eye, as is the plank, and both are quite easily removed if you but invite him to gently put his finger into your eye and pluck them out.

Your willingness to give up your sense of separation from your fellow humans and from God is the only way to take away the pain of the world so that *every tear shall be wiped away,* as promised in the book of Revelation. The key is to forgive others, yourself, and the world—the whole thing, even Jesus and God Himself if you still hold a grievance in your mind from years of misunderstanding their relationship to you. "A forgiven world rises before your eyes in innocence and majesty, to bring the face of Christ in every brother," says *ACIM*.

As *D.U.* states in its pages, the apparent suffering that ensues whenever we embark on a path of self-transformation and enlightenment is merely the unconscious guilt that surfaces now in order to be forgiven. I had misunderstood the stormy nights that came forth after beginning my work with *The Course* as indicators of failure, when in reality they heralded the truth that I was really doing nothing more than learning how to face the makings of my own ego, and that's what needed to be healed.

That's ultimately what needs to be forgiven so that *your* total innocence is remembered. You don't effectively welcome Jesus as a personal savior until you're ready to forgive yourself and then do so effectively. You can't give of what you don't have. An empty vessel can't offer water to those who thirst; it must first fill itself with water, which it can then give and pour abundantly. To receive forgiveness, one must forgive. To receive peace, one must first choose it.

Yes, the little girl in the story was me. I'm eternally grateful to the Foundation for Inner Peace for publishing *A Course in Miracles,* the answer from God through His voice in Jesus, our brother. It all makes sense now. As a child I asked my questions of God and then saw the luminescence through the Kirlian camera—the answer given by God. It was provided then and there.

At the exact same time that Judith Skutch Whitson, the hand that bore the responsibility for publishing *A Course in Miracles,* was getting acquainted with its original manuscript and was beginning its process of publication, I'd been looking into the Kirlian camera and other related psychic phenomena. In *Journey Without Distance,* Robert Skutch describes the process by which *ACIM* became a published work and some of the anecdotal circumstances surrounding its founding participants. This includes Judith Skutch's reference to her interest in the paranormal and the Kirlian camera phenomenon around the time of *ACIM*'s publication.

It's interesting to consider the simultaneity of these occurrences in time, though in space we were in different countries, cultures, languages, and stages of life. But in God's time we were both the same, because in Him, there's no time, distance, or differences. A distressed call from one of His children is always heard and answered. Perhaps we were both connecting to that answer through the same Spirit-Mind of which we are each an aspect.

Yet it took some 25 to 30 years for me to truly hear the answer and to realize the connection in hindsight—not because of where God is, but because of where I thought I was. Listening to His response meant learning a new language and immersing myself in its culture and literature, spiritual or otherwise, in order to shape my mind to really grasp the reply once it came, as indeed it has.

This is how things work sometimes, even as they bring along many forgiveness lessons. The answer was contained in these words from *The Course,* and it's my hope that reading the quotes that follow in Part II will help you connect to the answer's meaning in your heart through living its teaching. It's in the practice and experience of this teaching that the answer is heard, not in its reading alone.

"Salvation is God's justice. It restores to your awareness the wholeness of the fragments you perceive as broken off and separate. And it is this that overcomes the fear of death. For separate fragments must decay and die, but wholeness is immortal. It remains forever and forever like its Creator, being one with Him. God's Judgment is His justice. Onto this—a Judgment wholly lacking in condemnation; an evaluation based entirely on love—you have projected your injustice, giving God the lens of warped perception through which you look. Now it belongs to Him and not to you. You are afraid of Him, and do not see that you hate and fear your Self as enemy.

"Pray for God's justice, and do not confuse His mercy with your own insanity. Perception can make whatever picture the mind desires to see. Remember this. In this lies either Heaven or hell, as you elect. God's justice points to Heaven just because it is entirely impartial. It accepts all evidence that is brought before it, omitting nothing and assessing nothing as separate and apart from all the rest.

"From this one standpoint does it judge, and this alone. Here all attack and condemnation becomes meaningless and indefensible. Perception rests, the mind is still, and light returns again. Vision is now restored. What had been lost has now been found. The peace of God descends on all the world, and we can see. And we can see!" (ACIM M-19.4:1 M-19.5:13)

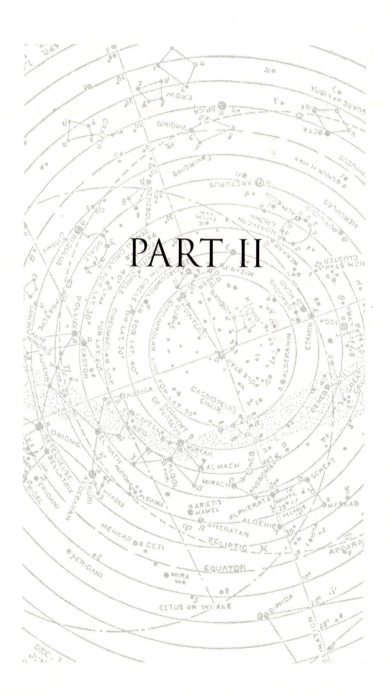

PART II

Spoken Miracles

The following are quotes from *A Course in Miracles (ACIM)* as presented in *The Disappearance of the Universe* by Gary R. Renard. Some words that appear in *ACIM* but not in the quoted text of *D.U.* have been added to complete the context of a phrase or paragraph. The chapters in this book are aligned with the titles of the chapters in *D.U.*

One of the things you will notice in the quotations from *ACIM* is that certain words seem to have been oddly capitalized and others are italicized. In *The Course,* words referring to activity of Divine origin or aspects of God are capitalized to distinguish God's realm from our human or worldly plane. Words are often italicized to emphasize their meaning and application.

I've included three pieces of information for each quote for easy referral back to *ACIM:*

1. The page on which it appears in *D.U.* (8th edition)

2. The endnote reference from *D.U.* (pages 410–412 in *D.U.*)

3. The *ACIM* location

Please use the following keys to interpret the *D.U.* end-note references and the *ACIM* locations.

D.U. Endnote References

In this reference, the first numeral listed is the footnote number from the chapter in which the quotation appeared in *D.U.*, followed by the standard designation of the page number of a quoted reference or direct paraphrase from *A Course in Miracles* or its two related pamphlets. Course references are written in *D.U.* as follows, with a letter denoting the book and a number denoting the page in that book:

Examples: T-459 = Text, *ACIM* page 459
W-104 = Workbook, *ACIM* page 104

The letters used are: T, W, M, PR, CL, P, and S. They stand for:

- **T**ext

- **W**orkbook for Students

- **M**anual for Teachers

- **Pr**eface

- **Cl**arification of Terms

- **P**sychotherapy: Purpose, Process, and Practice pamphlet

- The **S**ong of Prayer pamphlet

All page numbers are for the second edition of *The Course,* printed 1992 and later.

ACIM Locations

This information differs from the *D.U.* references because in standard *ACIM* nomenclature, quotes are usually given in one of two formats. The format used in *D.U.,* which offers section letter and page number, is typically used to refer to the first edition of *ACIM,* which did not contain paragraph and line numberings. This reference style was used in the beginning, during the first edition of *The Course,* since it wasn't numbered line by line.

The second edition contained paragraph and line numbering for easier reference to specific passages. The references to *ACIM* in *D.U.* use the first edition's reference style with the second edition's actual page numbers.

Annotation style for the second edition of *ACIM* is consistent with its paragraph and line numbering system as follows, and this is the style that I'm using for the *ACIM* locations in this compilation of quotes from *D.U.*

Abbreviations used:

- **T** = Text

- **W** = Workbook for Students

- **M** = Manual for Teachers

- **C** = Clarification of Terms

- **In** = Introduction

- **Pr** = Preface

- **r** = Review (workbook)

- **FL** = Final Lessons

- **Ep** = Epilogue

- **P** = Psychotherapy: Purpose, Process, and Practice pamphlet

- **S** = The Song of Prayer pamphlet

Annotation Examples:

- **T-22.V.1.3:6.** This points to the line found in Text, Chapter 22, Section V (*Note:* In the Text, chapter subsections are expressed in Roman numerals), Paragraph 1, Lines 3 to 6.

- **W-153.1.2.** This points to the line found in the Workbook for Students, Lesson 153, Paragraph 1, Line 2.

- **M-11.4.3.** This points to the line found in the Manual for Teachers, Question 11, Paragraph 4, Line 3.

CHAPTER 5

About the Appearance of Messengers

Day 1

There are those who have reached God directly, retaining no trace of worldly limits and remembering their own Identity perfectly. These might be called the Teachers of teachers because, although they are no longer visible, their image can yet be called upon. And they will appear when and where it is helpful for them to do so. To those to whom such appearances would be frightening, they give their ideas. No one can call on them in vain. Nor is there anyone of whom they are unaware.

D.U. ref.: 1. M64, *D.U.* page xix, *ACIM* location: M-26.2

Day 2

Communication is not limited to the small range of channels the world recognizes.

D.U. ref.: 2. M62, *D.U.* page 3, *ACIM* location: M-25.2.2

CHAPTER 6

About the Kingdom of God

Day 3

Be vigilant only for God and His Kingdom.

D.U. ref.: 1. T109, *D.U.* page 19, *ACIM* location: T-6.V.C

Day 4

"You also believe the body's brain can think."
". . . it is His Mind with which you Think."

D.U. ref.: 2. W159, *D.U.* pages 21–22, *ACIM* location: W-92.2,
W-92.3

Day 5

"Yet would I offer you my body, you whom I love,
knowing its littleness?"

D.U. ref.: 3. T411, *D.U.* page 22, *ACIM* location: T-19.IV.i.17.5

Day 6

[Guided by the Holy Spirit, the body] becomes a means by which the part of the mind you tried to separate from spirit can reach beyond its distortions and return to spirit.

D.U. ref.: 4. T153, *D.U.* page 36, *ACIM* location: T-8.VII.9.5

Day 7

In this world, because the mind is split, the Sons of God appear to be separate. Nor do their minds seem to be joined. In this illusory state, the concept of an "individual mind" seems to be meaningful. It is therefore described in the course as if it has two parts; spirit and ego.

Spirit is the part that is still in contact with God through the Holy Spirit, Who abides in this part but sees the other part as well. The term "soul" is not used except in direct biblical quotations because of its highly controversial nature. It would, however, be an equivalent of "spirit," with the understanding that, being of God, it is eternal and was never born.

The other part of the mind is entirely illusory and makes only illusions.

D.U. ref.: 5. L79, *D.U.* page 36, *ACIM* location: C-1.2

Day 8

You are merely asked to return to God the mind as He created it.

D.U. ref.: 6. T89, *D.U.* page 47, *ACIM* location: T-5.VII.2.6

Day 9

We say "God is," and then we cease to speak, for in that knowledge words are meaningless.

D.U. ref.: 7. W323, *D.U.* page 49, *ACIM* location: W-169.5.4

Day 10

The Holy Spirit wants only this, [to teach His pupils all He knows], for sharing the Father's Love for His Son, He seeks to remove all guilt from his mind that he may remember his Father in peace.

D.U. ref.: 8. T237, *D.U.* page 57, *ACIM* location: T-13.I.1:2

Day 11

Only acceptance can be asked of you, for what you are is certain. It is set forever in the holy Mind of God, and in your own.

D.U. ref.: 9. W268, *D.U.* page 79, *ACIM* location: W-139.8

Day 12

All that is given you is for release; the sight, the vision and the inner Guide all lead you out of hell with those you love beside you, and the universe with them.

D.U. ref.: 10. T664, *D.U.* page 86, *ACIM* location: T-31.VII.7.7

CHAPTER 7

About Miracles

Day 13

Miracles fall like drops of healing rain from Heaven on a dry and dusty world, where starved and thirsty creatures come to die.

D.U. ref.: 1. W473, *D.U.* page 87, *ACIM* location: W-pII.13.5

Day 14

To teach is to demonstrate.

D.U. ref.: 2. M1, *D.U.* page 91, *ACIM* location: M-in.2.

Day 15

Here are the laws that rule the world you made. And yet they govern nothing, and need not be broken; merely looked upon and gone beyond.

The first *chaotic* law is that the truth is different for everyone. Like all these principles, this one maintains that each is separate and has a different set of thoughts that set him off from others. This principle evolves from the belief there is a hierarchy of illusions; some are more valuable and therefore true.

D.U. ref.: 3. T489, *D.U.* pages 91–92, *ACIM* location: T-23.II.1.6–T-23.II.2.3

Day 16

This is a course in mind training.

D.U. ref.: 4. T16, *D.U.* page 93, *ACIM* location: T-1.VII.4.1

Day 17

An untrained mind can accomplish nothing.

D.U. ref.: 5. W1, *D.U.* page 93, *ACIM* location: W-in.1.3

Day 18

"there must be another way"

D.U. ref.: 6. PR vii, *D.U.* page 94, *ACIM* location: Preface vii

Day 19

There are no accidents in salvation.

D.U. ref.: 7. M7, *D.U.* page 94, *ACIM* location: M-3.1.6

Day 20

His is the Voice for God, and has therefore taken form. This form is not His reality, which God alone knows along with Christ, His real Son, Who is part of Him.

D.U. ref.: 8. CL89, *D.U.* page 97, *ACIM* location: C-6.1.4

Day 21

It seems as if things are being taken away, and it is rarely understood initially that their lack of value is merely being recognized.

D.U. ref.: 9. M10, *D.U.* page 98, *ACIM* location: M-4.I.A.3.3

Day 22

A sense of separation from God is the only lack you really need correct.

D.U. ref.: 10. T14, *D.U.* page 98, *ACIM* location: T-1.VI.2

Day 23

There is nothing about me that you cannot attain. I have nothing that does not come from God. The difference between us now is that I have nothing else.

D.U. ref.: 11. T7, *D.U.* page 99, *ACIM* location: T-1.II.3.10:12

Day 24

As we go along, you may have many "light episodes." They may take many different forms, some of them quite unexpected. Do not be afraid of them. They are signs that you are opening your eyes at last. They will not persist, because they merely symbolize true perception, and they are not related to knowledge.

D.U. ref.: 12. W25, *D.U.* page 102, *ACIM* location: W-15.3

Day 25

A sense of separation from God is the only lack you really need correct.

D.U. ref.: 13. T14, *D.U.* page 102, *ACIM* location: T-1.VI.2

Day 26

It is possible to do this all at once because there is but one shift in perception that is necessary, for you made but one mistake.

D.U. ref.: 14. T325, *D.U.* page 103, *ACIM* location: T-15.X.4.2

Day 27

The miracle is the only device at your immediate disposal for controlling time.

D.U. ref.: 15. T6, *D.U.* page 103, *ACIM* location: T-1.I.48

Day 28

The miracle substitutes for learning that might have taken thousands of years.

D.U. ref.: 16. T8, *D.U.* page 103, *ACIM* location: T-1.II.6.7

Day 29

The world you see is an illusion of a world. God did not create it, for what He creates must be eternal as Himself. Yet there is nothing in the world you see that will endure forever.

D.U. ref.: 17. CL85, *D.U.* page 104, *ACIM* location: C-4.1

Day 30

Whatever is true is eternal, and cannot change or be changed. Spirit is therefore unalterable because it is already perfect, but the mind can elect what it chooses to serve. The only limit put on its choice is that it cannot serve two masters.

D.U. ref.: 18. T13, *D.U.* page 104, *ACIM* location: T-1.V.5

Day 31

A theoretical foundation such as the text provides is necessary as a framework to make the exercises in this workbook meaningful.

D.U. ref.: 19. W1, *D.U.* page 106, *ACIM* location: W-in.1

Day 32

Some of the ideas the workbook presents you will find hard to believe, and others may seem to be quite startling. This does not matter. You are merely asked to apply the ideas as you are directed to do. You are not asked to judge them at all. You are asked only to use them. It is their use that will give them meaning to you, and will show you that they are true.

D.U. ref.: 20. W2, *D.U.* page 106, *ACIM* location: W-in.8

Day 33

To learn this course requires willingness to question every value that you hold.

D.U. ref.: 21. T499, *D.U.* page 107, *ACIM* location: T-24.in.2

Day 34

This is A Course in Miracles. It is a required course. Only the time you take it is voluntary. Free will does not mean that you can establish the curriculum. It means only that you can elect what you want to take at a given time. The course does not aim at teaching the meaning of love, for that is beyond what can be taught. It does aim, however, at removing the blocks to the awareness of love's presence, which is your natural inheritance. The opposite of love is fear, but what is all-encompassing can have no opposite.

This course can therefore be summed up very simply in this way:

Nothing real can be threatened.
Nothing unreal exists.
Herein lies the peace of God.

D.U. ref.: 22. T1, *D.U.* page 107, *ACIM* location: T-in.1, T-in.2

Day 35

The Holy Spirit and the ego are the only choices open to you.

D.U. ref.: 23. T85, *D.U.* page 108, *ACIM* location: T-5.V.6.8

Day 36

For the special love relationship, in which the meaning of love is hidden, is undertaken solely to offset the hate, but not to let it go.

D.U. ref.: 24. T337, *D.U.* page 108, *ACIM* location: T-16.IV.1.3

Day 37

No one can escape from illusions unless he looks at them, for not looking is the way they are protected.

D.U. ref.: 25. T202, *D.U.* page 108, *ACIM* location: T-11.V.1

Day 38

. . . the separation was and is dissociation, and once it occurs projection becomes its main defense, or the device that keeps it going. The reason, however, may not be so obvious as you think.

What you project you disown, and therefore do not believe is yours. You are excluding yourself by the very judgment that you are different from the one on whom you project. Since you have also judged against what you project, you continue to attack it because you continue to keep it separated. By doing this unconsciously, you try to keep the fact that you attacked yourself out of awareness, and thus imagine that you have made yourself safe.

Yet projection will always hurt you. It reinforces your belief in your own split mind, and its only purpose is to keep the separation going. It is solely a device of the ego to make you feel different from your brothers and separated from them. The ego justifies this on the grounds that it makes you seem "better" than they are, thus obscuring your equality with them still further. Projection and attack are inevitably related, because projection is always a means of justifying attack. Anger without projection is impossible. The ego uses projection only to destroy your perception of both yourself and your brothers. The process begins by excluding something that exists in you but which you do not want, and leads directly to excluding you from your brothers.

D.U. ref.: 26. T96, *D.U.* page 108, *ACIM* location: T-6.II.1.5, T-6.II.2, T-6.II.3.

Day 39

Knowledge is not the motivation for learning this course. Peace is. This is the prerequisite for knowledge only because those who are in conflict are not peaceful, and peace is the condition of knowledge because it is the condition of the Kingdom. Knowledge can be restored only when you meet its conditions.

D.U. ref.: 27. T138, *D.U.* page 109, *ACIM* location: T-8.I.1

Day 40

Complete abstraction is the natural condition of the mind.

D.U. ref.: 28. W304, *D.U.* page 109, *ACIM* location: W-161.2

Day 41

The Holy Spirit abides in the part of your mind that is part of the Christ Mind. He represents your Self and your Creator, Who are One. He speaks for God and also for you, being joined with Both. And therefore it is He Who proves Them One. He seems to be a Voice, for in that form He speaks God's Word to you. He seems to be a Guide through a far country, for you need that form of help.

D.U. ref.: 29. CL89, *D.U.* page 110, *ACIM* location: C-6.4

Day 42

The guiltless mind cannot suffer.

D.U. ref.: 30. T84, *D.U.* page 111, *ACIM* location: T-5.V.5

Day 43

Innocence is not a partial attribute. It is not real until it is total. The partly innocent are apt to be quite foolish at times. It is not until their innocence becomes a viewpoint with universal application that it becomes wisdom. Innocent or true perception means that you never misperceive and always see truly.

D.U. ref.: 31. T38, *D.U.* page 112, *ACIM* location: T-3.II.2

Day 44

We have distorted the world by our twisted defenses, and are therefore seeing what is not there.

D.U. ref.: 32. PR xi, *D.U.* page 112, *ACIM* location: Preface xi

Day 45

There can be no salvation in the dream as you are dreaming it.

D.U. ref.: 33. T623, *D.U.* page 112, *ACIM* location: T-29.IX.4

Day 46

Some of the ideas the workbook presents you will find hard to believe, and others may seem to be quite startling. This does not matter. You are merely asked to apply the ideas as you are directed to do. You are not asked to judge them at all. You are asked only to use them. It is their use that will give them meaning to you, and will show you that they are true.

D.U. ref.: 34. W2, *D.U.* page 113, *ACIM* location: W-in.8

Day 47

What is the ego? But a dream of what you really are. A thought you are apart from your Creator and a wish to be what He created not. It is a thing of madness, not reality at all. A name for namelessness is all it is. A symbol of impossibility; a choice for options that do not exist. We name it but to help us understand that it is nothing but an ancient thought that what is made has immortality.

D.U. ref.: 35. CL81, *D.U.* page 113, *ACIM* location: C-2.1

Day 48

That is why the Bible speaks of "the peace of God which passeth understanding." This peace is totally incapable of being shaken by errors of any kind. It denies the ability of anything not of God to affect you. This is the proper use of denial.

D.U. ref.: 36. T19, *D.U.* page 114, *ACIM* location: T-2.II.1.9

Day 49

Forgiveness, then, is an illusion, but because of its purpose, which is the Holy Spirit's, it has one difference. Unlike all other illusions it leads away from error and not towards it.

D.U. ref.: 37. CL83, *D.U.* page 114, *ACIM* location: C-3.1

Day 50

I undertook to show this was true in an extreme case, merely because it would serve as a good teaching aid to those whose temptation to give in to anger and assault would not be so extreme. I will with God that none of His Sons should suffer.

D.U. ref.: 38. T94, *D.U.* page 114, *ACIM* location: T-6.I.11.6

Day 51

He has established Jesus as the leader in carrying out His plan since he was the first to complete his own part perfectly. All power in Heaven and earth is therefore given him and he will share it with you when you have completed yours.

D.U. ref.: 39. CL89, *D.U.* page 114, *ACIM* location: C-6.2.2

Day 52

This is a course in cause and not effect.

D.U. ref.: 40. T463, *D.U.* page 115, *ACIM* location: T-21.VII.7.8

Day 53

Therefore, seek not to change the world, but choose to change your mind about the world.

D.U. ref.: 41. T445, *D.U.* page 115, *ACIM* location: T-21.in.1.7

Day 54

Do you prefer that you be right or happy?

D.U. ref.: 42. T617, *D.U.* page 115, *ACIM* location: T-29.VII.1.9

Day 55

Would you join in the resurrection or the crucifixion? Would you condemn your brothers or free them? Would you transcend your prison and ascend to the Father? These questions are all the same, and are answered together. There has been much confusion about what perception means, because the word is used both for awareness and for the interpretation of awareness. Yet you cannot be aware without interpretation, for what you perceive is your interpretation.

D.U. ref.: 43. T207, *D.U.* page 116, *ACIM* location: T-11.VI.2

Day 56

There is no challenge to a teacher of God. Challenge implies doubt, and the trust on which God's teachers rest secure makes doubt impossible.

D.U. ref.: 44. M12, *D.U.* page 116, *ACIM* location: M-4.II.2.5

Day 57

The miracle compares what you have made with creation, accepting what is in accord with it as true, and rejecting what is out of accord as false.

D.U. ref.: 45. T6, *D.U.* page 117, *ACIM* location: T-1.I.50

Day 58

All terms are potentially controversial, and those who seek controversy will find it. Yet those who seek clarification will find it as well. They must, however, be willing to overlook controversy, recognizing that it is a defense against truth in the form of a delaying maneuver.

D.U. ref.: 46. CL77, *D.U.* page 117, *ACIM* location: C-in.2

Day 59

Although Christian in statement, the Course deals with universal spiritual themes. It emphasizes that it is but one version of the universal curriculum. There are many others, this one differing from them only in form. They all lead to God in the end.

D.U. ref.: 47. PR ix, *D.U.* page 117, *ACIM* location: Preface ix

Day 60

It can indeed be said the ego made its world on sin. Only in such a world could everything be upside down. This is the strange illusion that makes the clouds of guilt seem heavy and impenetrable. The solidness that this world's foundation seems to have is found in this. For sin has changed creation from an Idea of God to an ideal the ego wants; a world it rules, made up of bodies, mindless and capable of complete corruption and decay. If this is a mistake, it can be undone easily by truth. Any mistake can be corrected, if truth be left to judge it. But if the mistake is given the status of truth, to what can it be brought?

D.U. ref.: 48. T403, *D.U.* page 118, *ACIM* location: T-19.II.6

CHAPTER 8

About the Secrets of Existence

Day 61

There is no life outside of Heaven. Where God created life, there life must be.

D.U. ref.: 1. T493, *D.U.* page 119, *ACIM* location: T-23.II.19

Day 62

The workbook is divided into two main sections, the first dealing with the undoing of the way you see now, and the second with the acquisition of true perception.

D.U. ref.: 2. W1, *D.U.* page 119, *ACIM* location: W-in.3

Day 63

A theoretical foundation such as the text provides is necessary as a framework to make the exercises in this workbook meaningful. Yet it is doing the exercises that will make the goal of the course possible.

D.U. ref.: 3. Ibid, *D.U.* page 120, *ACIM* location: W-in.1

Day 64

Only very few can hear God's Voice at all . . .

D.U. ref.: 4. M31, *D.U.* page 120, *ACIM* location: M-12.3.3

Day 65

There is no statement that the world is more afraid to hear than this:

I do not know the thing I am, and therefore do not know what I am doing, where I am, or how to look upon the world or on myself.

Yet in this learning is salvation born. And What you are will tell you of Itself.

D.U. ref.: 5. T660, *D.U.* page 121, *ACIM* location: T-31.V.17.6

Day 66

You travel but in dreams, while safe at home.

D.U. ref.: 6. T257, *D.U.* page 124, *ACIM* location: T-13.VII.17.7

Day 67

Into eternity, where all is one, there crept a tiny, mad idea, at which the Son of God remembered not to laugh.

D.U. ref.: 7. T586, *D.U.* page 124, *ACIM* location: T-27.VIII.6.2

Day 68

The Holy Spirit is in you in a very literal sense. His is the Voice that calls you back to where you were before and will be again.

D.U. ref.: 8. T75, *D.U.* page 125, *ACIM* location: T-5.II.3.7

Day 69

If this were the real world, God *would* be cruel. For no Father could subject His children to this as the price of salvation and *be* loving.

D.U. ref.: 9. T236, *D.U.* page 125, *ACIM* location: T-13.in.3

Day 70

You are a miracle, capable of creating in the likeness of your Creator. Everything else is your own nightmare, and does not exist.

D.U. ref.: 10. T4, *D.U.* page 126, *ACIM* location: T-1.I.24.3

Day 71

You are at home in God, dreaming of exile but perfectly capable of awakening to reality.

D.U. ref.: 11. T182, *D.U.* page 127, *ACIM* location: T-10.I.2

Day 72

Consciousness, the level of perception, was the first split introduced into the mind after the separation, making the mind a perceiver rather than a creator. Consciousness is correctly identified as the domain of the ego.

D.U. ref.: 12. T42, *D.U.* page 129, *ACIM* location: T-3.IV.2

Day 73

Perception did not exist until the separation introduced degrees, aspects and intervals. Spirit has no levels, and all conflict arises from the concept of levels.

D.U. ref.: 13. Ibid, *D.U.* page 129, *ACIM* location: T-3.IV.1.5

Day 74

Perception always involves some misuse of mind, because it brings the mind into areas of uncertainty.

D.U. ref.: 14. Ibid, *D.U.* page 130, *ACIM* location: T-3.IV.5

Day 75

In His function as Interpreter of what you made, the Holy Spirit uses special relationships, which you have chosen to support the ego, as learning experiences that point to truth. Under His teaching, every relationship becomes a lesson in love.

D.U. ref.: 15. T312, *D.U.* page 130, *ACIM* location: T-15.V.4.5:6

Day 76

The ego is nothing more than a part of your belief about yourself.

D.U. ref.: 16. T67, *D.U.* page 132, *ACIM* location: T-4.VI.1.6

Day 77

The Holy Spirit came into being with the separation as a protection, inspiring the Atonement principle at the same time.

D.U. ref.: 17. T74, *D.U.* page 133, *ACIM* location: T-5.I.5.2

Day 78

He tells you to return your whole mind to God, because it has never left Him. If it has never left Him, you need only perceive it as it is to be returned. The full awareness of the

Atonement, then, is the recognition that *the separation never occurred*.

D.U. ref.: 18. T98, *D.U.* page 133, *ACIM* location: T-6.II.10.5

Day 79

The ego must offer you some sort of reward for maintaining this belief. [The belief that the separation did occur.] All it can offer is a sense of temporary existence, which begins with its own beginning and ends with its own ending. It tells you this life is your existence because it is its own.

D.U. ref.: 19. T60, *D.U.* page 133, *ACIM* location: T-4.III.3.3

Day 80

You do not realize the magnitude of that one error. It was so vast and so completely incredible that from it a world of total unreality *had* to emerge. What else could come of it? Its fragmented aspects are fearful enough, as you begin to look at them. But nothing you have seen begins to show you the enormity of the original error, which seemed to cast you out of Heaven, to shatter knowledge into meaningless bits of disunited perceptions, and to force you to make further substitutions.

D.U. ref.: 20. T373, *D.U.* page 135, *ACIM* location: T-18.I.5.2

Day 81

I am not a victim of the world I see.
I have invented the world I see.

D.U. ref.: 21. W48, *D.U.* page 135, *ACIM* location: W-31, W-32

Day 82

The ego's voice is an hallucination. You cannot expect it to say "I am not real." Yet you are not asked to dispel your hallucinations alone.

D.U. ref.: 22. T138, *D.U.* page 136, *ACIM* location: T-8.I.2.2

Day 83

Against this sense of temporary existence spirit offers you the knowledge of permanence and unshakable being. No one who has experienced the revelation of this can ever fully believe in the ego again. How can its meager offering to you prevail against the glorious gift of God?

D.U. ref.: 23. T60–61, *D.U.* page 136, *ACIM* location: T-4.III.3.6

Day 84

The course does not aim at teaching the meaning of love, for that is beyond what can be taught. It does aim, however, at removing the blocks to the awareness of love's presence, which is your natural inheritance.

D.U. ref.: 24. T1, *D.U.* page 136, *ACIM* location: T-in.1.6

Day 85

Freedom from illusions lies only in not believing them.

D.U. ref.: 25. T154, *D.U.* page 139, *ACIM* location: T-8.VII.16.5

Day 86

The opposite of love is fear, but what is all-encompassing can have no opposite.

D.U. ref.: 26. T1, *D.U.* page 139, *ACIM* location: T-in.1.8

Day 87

Here is your promise never to allow union to call you out of separation; the great amnesia in which the memory of God seems quite forgotten; the cleavage of your Self from you;—*the fear of God*, the final step in your dissociation.

D.U. ref.: 27. T420, *D.U.* page 141, *ACIM* location: T-19.IV.D.3.4

Day 88

The ego is the part of the mind that believes in division. How could part of God detach itself without believing it is attacking Him? We spoke before of the authority problem as based on the concept of usurping God's power. The ego believes that this is what you did because it believes that it is you. If you identify with the ego, you must perceive yourself as guilty. Whenever you respond to your ego you will experience guilt, and you will fear punishment. The ego is quite literally a fearful thought. However ridiculous the idea of attacking God may be to the sane mind, never forget that the ego is not sane. It represents a delusional system, and speaks for it. Listening to the ego's voice means that you believe it is possible to attack God, and that a part of Him has been torn away by you. Fear of retaliation from without follows, because the severity of the guilt is so acute that it must be projected.

D.U. ref.: 28. T84, *D.U.* page 141, *ACIM* location: T-5.V.3

Day 89

No one can escape from illusions unless he looks at them, for not looking is the way they are protected. There is no need to shrink from illusions, for they cannot be dangerous. We are ready to look more closely at the ego's thought system because together we have the lamp that will dispel it, and since you realize you do not want it, you must be ready. Let us be very calm in doing this, for we are merely looking honestly for truth. The "dynamics" of the ego will be our lesson for a while, for we must look first at this to see beyond it, since you have made it real. We will undo this error quietly together, and then look beyond it to truth.

D.U. ref.: 29. T202, *D.U.* page 144, *ACIM* location: T-11.V.1

Day 90

Knowledge must precede dissociation, so that dissociation is nothing more than a decision to forget. What has been forgotten then appears to be fearful, but only because the dissociation is an attack on truth.

D.U. ref.: 30. T183, *D.U.* page 145, *ACIM* location: T-10.II.1.2

Day 91

Can you be separated from your identification and be at peace? Dissociation is not a solution; it is a delusion. The delusional believe that truth will assail them, and they do not recognize it because they prefer the delusion. Judging truth as something they do not want, they perceive their illusions which block knowledge.

D.U. ref.: 31. T146, *D.U.* page 145, *ACIM* location: T-8.V.1

Day 92

Escape from judgment simply lies in this; all things have but one purpose, which you share with all the world.

And nothing in the world can be opposed to it, for it belongs to everything, as it belongs to you. In single purpose is the end of all ideas of sacrifice, which must assume a different purpose for the one who gains and him who loses. There could be no thought of sacrifice apart from this idea. And it is this idea of different goals that makes perception shift and meaning change. In one united goal does this become impossible, for your agreement makes interpretation stabilize and last.

How can communication really be established while the symbols that are used mean different things? The Holy Spirit's goal gives one interpretation, meaningful to you and to your brother. Thus can you communicate with him, and he with you. In symbols that you both can understand the sacrifice of meaning is undone. All sacrifice entails the loss of your ability to see relationships among events. And looked at separately they have no meaning. For there is no light by which they can be seen and understood. They have no purpose. And what they are for cannot be seen. In any thought of loss there is no meaning. No one has agreed with you on what it means. It is a part of a distorted script, which cannot be interpreted with meaning. It must be forever unintelligible. This is not communication. Your dark dreams are but the senseless, isolated scripts you write in sleep. Look not to separate dreams for meaning. Only dreams of pardon can be shared. They mean the same to both of you.

D.U. ref.: 32. T641–642, *D.U.* page 146, *ACIM* location: T-30.VII.5–T-30.VII.6

Day 93

We merely take the part assigned long since, and fully recognized as perfectly fulfilled by Him Who wrote salvation's script in His Creator's Name, and in the Name of His Creator's Son.

D.U. ref.: 33. W324, *D.U.* page 147, *ACIM* location: W-PI.169.9.3

Day 94

Truth does not vacillate; it is always true.

D.U. ref.: 34. T179, *D.U.* page 147, *ACIM* location: T-9.VIII.7.2

Day 95

This is not a course in philosophical speculation, nor is it concerned with precise terminology. It is concerned only with Atonement, or the correction of perception. The means of the Atonement is forgiveness.

D.U. ref.: 35. CL77, *D.U.* page 147, *ACIM* location: C-in.1.1

Day 96

An idol is established by belief, and when it is withdrawn the idol "dies." This is the anti-Christ; the strange idea there is a power past omnipotence, a place beyond the infinite, a time transcending the eternal. Here the world of idols has been set by the idea this power and place and time are given form, and shape the world where the impossible has happened. Here the deathless come to die, the all-encompassing to suffer loss, the timeless to be made the slaves of time. Here does the changeless change; the peace of God, forever given to all living things, give way to chaos. And the Son of God, as perfect, sinless and as loving as his Father, come to hate a little while; to suffer pain and finally to die.

D.U. ref.: 36. T620–621, *D.U.* page 148, *ACIM* location: T-29.VIII.6

Day 97

The truth about you is so lofty that nothing unworthy of God is worthy of you. Choose, then, what you want in these terms, and accept nothing that you would not offer to God as wholly fitting for Him.

D.U. ref.: 37. T177, *D.U.* page 151, *ACIM* location: T-9.VII.8.4

Day 98

If you want to be like me I will help you, knowing that we are alike. If you want to be different, I will wait until you change your mind.

D.U. ref.: 38. T145, *D.U.* page 151, *ACIM* location: T-8.IV.6.3

CHAPTER 9

About the Ego's Plan

Day 99

Every response to the ego is a call to war, and war does deprive you of peace. Yet in this war there is no opponent.

D.U. ref.: 1. T138, *D.U.* page 153, *ACIM* location: T-8.I.3

Day 100

To forgive is merely to remember only the loving thoughts you gave in the past, and those that were given you. All the rest must be forgotten. Forgiveness is a selective remembering, based not on your selection. For the shadow figures you would make immortal are "enemies" of reality. Be willing to forgive the Son of God for what he did not do. The shadow figures are the witnesses you bring with you to demonstrate he did what he did not.

D.U. ref.: 2. T354, *D.U.* page 155, *ACIM* location: T-17.III.1

Day 101

You have been told not to make error real, and the way to do this is very simple. If you want to believe in error, you would have to make it real because it is not true. But truth is real in its own right, and to believe in truth *you do not have to do anything.* Understand that you do not respond to anything directly, but to your interpretation of it. Your interpretation thus becomes the justification for the response. That is why analyzing the motives of others is hazardous to you. If you decide that someone is really trying to attack you or desert you or enslave you, you will respond as if he had actually done so, having made his error real to you. To interpret error is to give it power, and having done this you will overlook truth.

D.U. ref.: 3. T215, *D.U.* page 155, *ACIM* location: T-12.I.1

Day 102

I am not the victim of the world I see.

D.U. ref.: 4. W48, *D.U.* page 155, *ACIM* location: W-PI.31

Day 103

Miracles are habits, and should be involuntary. They should not be under conscious control. Consciously selected miracles can be misguided.

D.U. ref.: 5. T3, *D.U.* page 158, *ACIM* location: T-1.I.5

Day 104

Love holds no grievances.

You who were created by love like Itself can hold no grievances and know your Self. To hold a grievance is to forget who you are. To hold a grievance is to see yourself as a body. To hold a grievance is to let the ego rule your mind and to condemn the body to death. Perhaps you do not yet fully realize just what holding grievances does to your mind. It seems to split you off from your Source and make you unlike Him. It makes you believe that He is like what you think you have become, for no one can conceive of his Creator as unlike himself.

Shut off from your Self, which remains aware of Its likeness to Its Creator, your Self seems to sleep, while the part of your mind that weaves illusions in its sleep appears to be awake. Can all this arise from holding grievances? Oh, yes! For he who holds grievances denies he was created by love, and his Creator has become fearful to him in his dream of hate. Who can dream of hatred and not fear God?

It is as sure that those who hold grievances will redefine God in their own image, as it is certain that God created them like Himself, and defined them as part of Him. It is as sure that those who hold grievances will suffer guilt, as it is certain that those who forgive will find peace. It is as sure that those who hold grievances will forget who they are, as it is certain that those who forgive will remember.

Would you not be willing to relinquish your grievances if you believed all this were so? Perhaps you do not think you can let your grievances go. That, however, is simply a matter of motivation.

D.U. ref.: 6. W115, *D.U.* page 158, *ACIM* location: W-68.1–W-68.4

Day 105

Let us be glad that we can walk the world, and find so many chances to perceive another situation where God's gift can once again be recognized as ours! And thus will all the vestiges of hell, the secret sins and hidden hates be gone.

D.U. ref.: 7. T668, *D.U.* page 159, *ACIM* location: T-31.VIII.9

Day 106

Seek not outside yourself. For all your pain comes simply from a futile search for what you want, insisting where it must be found. What if it is not there? Do you prefer that you be right or happy? Be you glad that you are told where happiness abides, and seek no longer elsewhere.

D.U. ref.: 8. T617, *D.U.* page 160, *ACIM* location: T-29.VII.1.6

Day 107

Temptation has one lesson it would teach, in all its forms, wherever it occurs. It would persuade the holy Son of God he is a body, born in what must die, unable to escape its frailty, and bound by what it orders him to feel.

D.U. ref.: 9. T666, *D.U.* page 160, *ACIM* location: T-31.VIII.1

Day 108

The light of truth is in us, where it was placed by God. It is the body that is outside us, and is not our concern. To be without a body is to be in our natural state. To recognize the light of truth in us is to recognize ourselves as we are. To see our Self as separate from the body is to end the attack on God's plan for salvation, and to accept it instead. And wherever His plan is accepted, it is accomplished already.

D.U. ref.: 10. W125, *D.U.* page 160, *ACIM* location: W-72.9

Day 109

The body is the ego's idol; the belief in sin made flesh and then projected outward. This produces what seems to be a wall of flesh around the mind, keeping it prisoner in a tiny spot of space and time, beholden unto death, and given but an instant in which to sigh and grieve and die in honor of its master. And this unholy instant seems to be life; an instant of despair, a tiny island of dry sand, bereft of water and set uncertainly upon oblivion.

D.U. ref.: 11. T438, *D.U.* page 161, *ACIM* location: T-20.VI.11

Day 110

. . . peace must first surmount the obstacle of your desire to get rid of it. Where the attraction of guilt holds sway, peace is not wanted. The second obstacle that peace must flow across, and closely related to the first, is the belief that the body is valuable for what it offers. For here is the attraction of guilt made manifest in the body, and seen in it.

D.U. ref.: 12. T412, *D.U.* page 161, *ACIM* location: T-19.IV.B.1

Day 111

The attraction of guilt produces fear of love, for love would never look on guilt at all. It is the nature of love to look upon only the truth, for there it sees itself, with which it would unite in holy union and completion. As love must look past fear, so must fear see love not. For love contains the end of guilt, as surely as fear depends on it. Love is attracted only to love. Overlooking guilt completely, it sees no fear. Being wholly without attack, it could not be afraid. Fear is attracted to what love sees not, and each believes that what the other looks upon does not exist. Fear looks on guilt with just the same devotion that love looks on itself. And each has messengers which it sends forth, and which return to it with messages written in the language in which their going forth was asked.

. . . The messengers of fear are harshly ordered to seek out guilt, and cherish every scrap of evil and of sin that they can find, losing none of them on pain of death, and laying them respectfully before their lord and master.

Is not this inevitable? Under fear's orders the body will pursue guilt, serving its master whose attraction to guilt maintains the whole illusion of its existence. This, then, is the attraction of pain. Ruled by this perception the body becomes the servant of pain, seeking it dutifully and obeying the idea that pain is pleasure. It is this idea that underlies all of the ego's heavy investment in the body. And it is this insane relationship that it keeps hidden, and yet feeds upon. To you it teaches that the body's pleasure is happiness. Yet to itself it whispers, "It is death."

D.U. ref.: 13. T410, 414–415, *D.U.* page 161, *ACIM* location: T-19.IV.A.10, T-19.IV.A.11.2, T-19.IV.B.13

Day 112

It is impossible to seek for pleasure through the body and not find pain. It is essential that this relationship be understood, for it is one the ego sees as proof of sin. It is not really punitive at all. It is but the inevitable result of equating yourself with the body, which is the invitation to pain. For it invites fear to enter and become your purpose. The attraction of guilt *must* enter with it, and whatever fear directs the body to do is therefore painful. It will share the pain of all illusions, and the illusion of pleasure will be the same as pain.

D.U. ref.: 14. T415, *D.U.* page 161, *ACIM* location: T-19.IV.B.12

Day 113

The miracle minimizes the need for time. In the longitudinal or horizontal plane the recognition of the equality of the members of the Sonship appears to involve almost endless time. However, the miracle entails a sudden shift from horizontal to vertical perception. This introduces an interval from which the giver and receiver both emerge farther along in time than they would otherwise have been. The miracle thus has the unique property of abolishing time to the extent that it renders the interval of time it spans unnecessary. There is no relationship between the time a miracle takes and the time it covers. The miracle substitutes for learning that might have taken thousands of years. It does so by the underlying recognition of perfect equality of giver and receiver on which the miracle rests. The miracle shortens time by collapsing it, thus eliminating certain intervals within it. It does this, however, within the larger temporal sequence.

D.U. ref.: 15. T8, *D.U.* page 162, *ACIM* location: T-1.II.6

Day 114

It is the figures in the dream and what they do that seem to make the dream. You do not realize that you are making them act out for you, for if you did the guilt would not be theirs, and the illusion of satisfaction would be gone. In dreams these features are not obscure. You seem to waken, and the dream is gone. Yet what you fail to recognize is that what caused the dream has not gone with it. Your wish to make another world that is not real remains with you. And what you seem to waken to is but another form of this same world you see in dreams. All your time is spent in dreaming. Your sleeping and your waking dreams have different forms, and that is all. Their content is the same.

D.U. ref.: 16. T376, *D.U.* page 164, *ACIM* location: T-18.II.5.5

Day 115

Yet the ego, though encouraging the search for love very actively, makes one proviso; do not find it. Its dictates, then, can be summed up simply as: "Seek and do *not* find." This is the one promise the ego holds out to you, and the one promise it will keep. For the ego pursues its goal with fanatic insistence, and its judgment, though severely impaired, is completely consistent.

D.U. ref.: 17. T223, *D.U.* page 165, *ACIM* location: T-12.IV.1.

Day 116

No one can escape from illusions unless he looks at them, for not looking is the way they are protected. There is no need to shrink from illusions, for they cannot be dangerous. We are ready to look more closely at the ego's thought system because together we have the lamp that will dispel it, and since you realize you do not want it, you must be ready.

D.U. ref.: 18. T202, *D.U.* page 167, *ACIM* location: T-11.V.1

Day 117

Fear and love are the only emotions of which you are capable. One is false, for it was made out of denial; and denial depends on the belief in what is denied for its own existence.

D.U. ref.: 19. T217, *D.U.* page 168, *ACIM* location: T-12.I.9.5

Day 118

Who sees a brother as a body sees him as fear's symbol. And he will attack, because what he beholds is his own fear external to himself, poised to attack, and howling to unite with him again. Mistake not the intensity of rage projected fear must spawn. It shrieks in wrath, and claws the air in frantic hope it can reach to its maker and devour him.

This do the body's eyes behold in one whom Heaven cherishes, the angels love and God created perfect.

D.U. ref.: 20. W305, *D.U.* page 170, *ACIM* location:
W-161.8–W-161.9

Day 119

Loudly the ego tells you not to look inward, for if you do your eyes will light on sin, and God will strike you blind.

D.U. ref.: 21. T454, *D.U.* page 170, *ACIM* location: T-21.IV.2

Day 120

Beneath your fear to look within because of sin is yet another fear, and one which makes the ego tremble.

What if you looked within and saw no sin? This "fearful" question is one the ego never asks. And you who ask it now are threatening the ego's whole defensive system too seriously for it to bother to pretend it is your friend.

D.U. ref.: 22. Ibid, *D.U.* page 170, *ACIM* location: T-21.IV.2.8–T-21.IV.3

Day 121

The world is not left by death but by truth, and truth can be known by all those for whom the Kingdom was created, and for whom it waits.

D.U. ref.: 23. T51, *D.U.* page 176, *ACIM* location: T-3.VII.6.11

Day 122

Anger is *never* justified. Attack has *no* foundation. It is here escape from fear begins, and will be made complete.

D.U. ref.: 24. T638, *D.U.* page 177, *ACIM* location: T-30.VI.1

Day 123

The secret of salvation is but this: that you are doing this unto yourself. No matter what the form of the attack, this still is true. Whoever takes the role of enemy and of attacker, still is this the truth. Whatever seems to be the cause of any pain and suffering you feel, this is still true. For you would not react at all to figures in a dream you knew that you were dreaming. Let them be as hateful and as vicious as they may, they could have no effect on you unless you failed to recognize it is your dream.

D.U. ref.: 25. T587–588, *D.U.* page 36, *ACIM* location: T-27.VIII.10

Day 124

You cannot dispel guilt by making it real, and then atoning for it. This is the ego's plan, which it offers instead of dispelling it. The ego believes in atonement through attack, being fully committed to the insane notion that attack is salvation.

D.U. ref.: 26. T239, *D.U.* page 178, *ACIM* location: T-13.I.10

Day 125

In the ego's teaching, then, there is no escape from guilt. For attack makes guilt real, and if it is real there *is* no way to overcome it.

D.U. ref.: 27. Ibid, *D.U.* page 178, *ACIM* location: T-13.I.11.2

Day 126

God does not forgive because He has never condemned. And there must be condemnation before forgiveness is necessary. Forgiveness is the great need of this world, but that is because it is a world of illusions. Those who forgive are thus releasing themselves from illusions, while those who withhold forgiveness are binding themselves to them. As you condemn only yourself, so do you forgive only yourself.

Yet although God does not forgive, His Love is nevertheless the basis of forgiveness.

D.U. ref.: 28. W73, *D.U.* page 178, *ACIM* location: W-46.1–W-46.2

Day 127

The Holy Spirit dispels it [guilt] simply through the calm recognition that it has never been.

D.U. ref.: 29. T239, *D.U.* page 179, *ACIM* location: T-13.I.11.4

Day 128

The body is the ego's idol; the belief in sin made flesh and then projected outward. This produces what seems to be a wall of flesh around the mind, keeping it prisoner in a tiny spot of space and time, beholden unto death, and given but an instant in which to sigh and grieve and die in honor of its master.

D.U. ref.: 30. T438, *D.U.* page 182, *ACIM* location: T-20.VI.11

Day 129

It is the figures in the dream and what they do that seem to make the dream. You do not realize that you are making them act out for you, for if you did the guilt would not be theirs, and the illusion of satisfaction would be gone.

D.U. ref.: 31. T376, *D.U.* page 185, *ACIM* location: T-18.II.5.5

Day 130

When you meet anyone, remember it is a holy encounter. As you see him you will see yourself. As you treat him you will treat yourself. As you think of him you will think of yourself. Never forget this, for in him you will find yourself or lose yourself. Whenever two Sons of God meet, they are given another chance at salvation. Do not leave anyone without giving salvation to him and receiving it yourself. For I am always there with you, in remembrance of *you.*

D.U. ref.: 32. T142, *D.U.* page 187, *ACIM* location: T-8.III.4

Day 131

The body appears to be largely self-motivated and independent, yet it actually responds only to the intentions of the mind.

D.U. ref.: 33. PR xii, *D.U.* page 189, *ACIM* location: Preface. Page xii, paragraph 3, sentence 3

Day 132

When you perform a miracle, I will arrange both time and space to adjust to it.

D.U. ref.: 34. T27, *D.U.* page 192, *ACIM* location: T-2.V.A.11.3

Day 133

The miracle shortens time by collapsing it, thus eliminating certain intervals within it. It does this, however, within the larger temporal sequence.

D.U. ref.: 35. T8, *D.U.* page 192, *ACIM* location: T-1.II.6.9

Day 134

For you are no longer wholly insane, and you would soon recognize the guilt of self-betrayal for what it is.

D.U. ref.: 36. T346, *D.U.* page 196, *ACIM* location: T-16.VI.8.8

Day 135

If you could recognize that your only problem is separation, no matter what form it takes, you could accept the answer because you would see its relevance.

D.U. ref.: 37. W14–142, *D.U.* page 198, *ACIM* location: W-79.6.2

Day 136

The ego, too, has a plan of forgiveness because you are asking for one, though not of the right teacher. The ego's plan, of course, makes no sense and will not work. By following its plan you will merely place yourself in an impossible situation, to which the ego always leads you. The ego's plan is to have you see error clearly first, and then overlook it. Yet how can you overlook what you have made real? By seeing it clearly, you have made it real and cannot overlook it.

D.U. ref.: 38. T169, *D.U.* page 201, *ACIM* location: T-9.IV.4

Day 137

Learn this, and learn it well, for it is here delay of happiness is shortened by a span of time you cannot realize. You never hate your brother for his sins, but only for your own. Whatever form his sins appear to take, it but obscures the fact that you believe them to be yours, and therefore meriting a "just" attack.

D.U. ref.: 39. T651, *D.U.* page 202, *ACIM* location: T-31.III.1.4

CHAPTER 10

About the Holy Spirit's Alternative

Day 138

The ego made the world as it perceives it, but the Holy Spirit, the reinterpreter of what the ego made, sees the world as a teaching device for bringing you home.

D.U. ref.: 1. T80, *D.U.* page 205, *ACIM* location: T-5.III.11

Day 139

His is the Voice for God, and has therefore taken form.

D.U. ref.: 2. CL89, *D.U.* page 208, *ACIM* location: C-6.1.4

Day 140

Today's idea but states the simple truth that makes the thought of sin impossible. It promises there is no cause for guilt, and being causeless it does not exist. It follows surely from the basic thought so often mentioned in the text; ideas leave not their source. If this be true, how can you be apart from God? How could you walk the world alone and separate from your Source?

D.U. ref.: 3. W294, *D.U.* page 208, *ACIM* location: W-156.1

Day 141

How else can you find joy in a joyless place except by realizing that you are not there?

D.U. ref.: 4. T97, *D.U.* page 210, *ACIM* location: T-6.II.6

Day 142

The difference between the ego's projection and the Holy Spirit's extension is very simple. The ego projects to exclude, and therefore to deceive. The Holy Spirit extends by recognizing Himself in every mind, and thus perceives them as one. Nothing conflicts in this perception, because what the Holy Spirit perceives is all the same. Wherever He looks He sees Himself, and because He is united He offers the whole Kingdom always. This is the one message God gave to Him and for which He must speak, because that is what He is. The peace of God lies in that message, and so the peace of God lies in you. The great peace of the Kingdom shines in your mind forever, but it must shine outward to make you aware of it.

D.U. ref.: 5. T98–99, *D.U.* page 210, *ACIM* location: T-6.II.12

Day 143

Forgive all thoughts which would oppose the truth of your completion, unity and peace. You cannot lose the gifts your Father gave.

D.U. ref.: 6. W178, *D.U.* page 211, *ACIM* location: W-99.10

Day 144

You but receive according to God's plan, and never lose or sacrifice or die.

D.U. ref.: 7. W181, *D.U.* page 211, *ACIM* location: W-100.7.7

Day 145

Only the self-accused condemn.

D.U. ref.: 8. T651, *D.U.* page 211, *ACIM* location: T-31.III.1

Day 146

You need not fear the Higher Court will condemn you. It will merely dismiss the case against you. There can be no case against a child of God, and every witness to guilt in God's creations is bearing false witness to God Himself. Appeal everything you believe gladly to God's Own Higher Court, because it speaks for Him and therefore speaks truly. It will dismiss the case against you, however carefully you have built it up. The case may be fool-proof, but it is not God-proof. The Holy Spirit will not hear it, because He can only witness truly. His verdict will always be "thine is the Kingdom," because He was given to you to remind you of what you are.

D.U. ref.: 9. T88, *D.U.* page 212, *ACIM* location: T-5.VI.10

Day 147

There is no world! This is the central thought the course attempts to teach. Not everyone is ready to accept it, and each one must go as far as he can let himself be led along the road to truth. He will return and go still farther, or perhaps step back a while and then return again.

But healing is the gift of those who are prepared to learn there is no world, and can accept the lesson now. Their readiness will bring the lesson to them in some form which they can understand and recognize.

D.U. ref.: 10. W243, *D.U.* page 212, *ACIM* location: W-132.6.2–W-132.7.2

Day 148

Having taught you to accept only loving thoughts in others and to regard everything else as an appeal for help, He has taught you that fear itself is an appeal for help. This is what recognizing fear really means. If you do not protect it, He will reinterpret it. That is the ultimate value in learning to perceive attack as a call for love. We have already learned that fear and attack are inevitably associated. If only attack produces fear, and if you see attack as the call for help that it is, the unreality of fear must dawn on you. For fear is a call for love, in unconscious recognition of what has been denied.

D.U. ref.: 11. T217, *D.U.* page 213, *ACIM* location: T-12.I.8.7-13

Day 149

What if you recognized this world is an hallucination? What if you really understood you made it up? What if you realized that those who seem to walk about in it, to sin and die, attack and murder and destroy themselves, are wholly unreal?

D.U. ref.: 12. T443, *D.U.* page 214, *ACIM* location: T-20.VIII.7.3

Day 150

Salvation is nothing more than "right-mindedness," which is not the One-mindedness of the Holy Spirit, but which must be achieved before One-mindedness is restored. Right-mindedness leads to the next step automatically, because right perception is uniformly without attack, and therefore wrong-mindedness is obliterated. The ego cannot survive without judgment, and is laid aside accordingly. The mind then has only one direction in which it can move. Its direction is always automatic, because it cannot but be dictated by the thought system to which it adheres.

D.U. ref.: 13. T59, *D.U.* page 215, *ACIM* location: T-4.II.10

Day 151

You dwell not here, but in eternity.

D.U. ref.: 14. T257, *D.U.* page 216, *ACIM* location: T-13.VII.17.6

Day 152

Whenever you are tempted to undertake a useless journey that would lead away from light, remember what you really want, and say:
The Holy Spirit leads me unto Christ, and where else would I go? What need have I but to awake in Him?

D.U. ref.: 15. Ibid, *D.U.* page 216, *ACIM* location: T-13.VII.14

Day 153

You cannot be hurt, and do not want to show your brother anything except your wholeness. Show him that he cannot hurt you and hold nothing against him, or you hold it against yourself. This is the meaning of "turning the other cheek."

D.U. ref.: 16. T82, *D.U.* page 216, *ACIM* location: T-5.IV.4.4

Day 154

Of one thing you were sure: Of all the many causes you perceived as bringing pain and suffering to you, your guilt was not among them.

D.U. ref.: 17. T583, *D.U.* page 217, *ACIM* location: T-27.VII.7.4

Day 155

The name of *Jesus* is the name of one who was a man but saw the face of Christ in all his brothers and remembered God. So he became identified with *Christ*, a man no longer, but at one with God.

D.U. ref.: 18. CL87, *D.U.* page 217, *ACIM* location: C-5.2

Day 156

It is the function of His Voice, His Holy Spirit, to mediate between the two worlds. He can do this because, while on the one hand He knows the truth, on the other He also recognizes our illusions, but without believing in them. It is the Holy Spirit's goal to help us escape from the dream world by teaching us how to reverse our thinking and unlearn our mistakes.

D.U. ref.: 19. PR xi, *D.U.* page 219, *ACIM* location: Preface xi.1.4–6

Day 157

The Holy Spirit understands the means you made, by which you would attain what is forever unattainable. And if you offer them to Him, He will employ the means you made for exile to restore your mind to where it truly is at home.

D.U. ref.: 20. W437, *D.U.* page 219, *ACIM* location: W-pII.7.3.2

Day 158

Jesus remains a Savior because he saw the false without accepting it as true.

D.U. ref.: 21. CL87, *D.U.* page 220, *ACIM* location: C-5.2.5

Day 159

The Holy Spirit abides in the part of your mind that is part of the Christ Mind.

D.U. ref.: 22. CL89, *D.U.* page 220, *ACIM* location: C-6.4

Day 160

He seems to be a Guide through a far country, for you need that form of help.

D.U. ref.: 23. Ibid, *D.U.* page 220, *ACIM* location: C-6.4.6

Day 161

You are not asked to make insane decisions, although you can think you are. It must, however, be insane to believe that it is up to you to decide what God's creations are. The Holy Spirit perceives the conflict exactly as it is. Therefore, His second lesson is: *To have peace, teach peace to learn it.*

This is still a preliminary step, since *having* and *being* are still not equated. It is, however, more advanced than the first step, which is really only the beginning of the thought reversal. The second step is a positive affirmation of what you want. This, then, is a step in the direction out of conflict, since it means that alternatives have been considered, and one has been chosen as more desirable. Nevertheless, the term "more desirable" still implies that the desirable has degrees. Therefore, although this step is essential for the ultimate decision, it is clearly not the final one.

D.U. ref.: 24. T108, *D.U.* page 220, *ACIM* location:
T-6.V.B.7–T-6.V.B.8.6

Day 162

Is not the escape of God's beloved Son from evil dreams that he imagines, yet believes are true, a worthy purpose? Who could hope for more, while there appears to be a choice to make between success and failure; love and fear?

D.U. ref.: 25. W384–385, *D.U.* page 221, *ACIM* location:
W-200.6.5

Day 163

As you share my unwillingness to accept error in yourself and others, you must join the great crusade to correct it; listen to my voice, learn to undo error and act to correct it. The power to work miracles belongs to you. I will provide the opportunities to do them, but you must be ready and willing. Doing them will bring conviction in the ability, because conviction comes through accomplishment. The ability is the potential, the achievement is its expression, and the Atonement, which is the natural profession of the children of God, is the purpose.

D.U. ref.: 26. T9, D.U. page 221, ACIM location: T-1.III.1.6-10

Day 164

Against the ego's insane notion of salvation the Holy Spirit gently lays the holy instant. We said before that the Holy Spirit must teach through comparisons, and uses opposites to point to truth. The holy instant is the opposite of the ego's fixed belief in salvation through vengeance for the past.

D.U. ref.: 27. T349, D.U. page 222, ACIM location: T-16.VII.6

Day 165

Faith makes the power of belief, and where it is invested determines its reward. For faith is always given what is treasured, and what is treasured is returned to you.

D.U. ref.: 28. T261, *D.U.* page 223, *ACIM* location: T-13.IX.2.5

Day 166

As you approach the Beginning, you feel the fear of the destruction of your thought system upon you as if it were the fear of death. There is no death, but there is a belief in death.

D.U. ref.: 29. T51, *D.U.* page 225, *ACIM* location: T-3.VII.5.10

Day 167

The sign of Christmas is a star, a light in darkness. See it not outside yourself, but shining in the Heaven within, and accept it as the sign the time of Christ has come.

D.U. ref.: 30. T327, *D.U.* page 225, *ACIM* location: T-15.XI.2

CHAPTER 11

About Forgiveness

Day 168

Fear binds the world. Forgiveness sets it free.

D.U. ref.: 1. W468, *D.U.* page 227, *ACIM* location: W-332-Title

Day 169

Yet there is no answer; only an experience. Seek only this, and do not let theology delay you.

D.U. ref.: 2. CL77, *D.U.* page 227, *ACIM* location: C-in.4.4:5

Day 170

You do not think of light in terms of strength, and darkness in terms of weakness. That is because your idea of what seeing means is tied up with the body and its eyes and brain. Thus you believe that you can change what you see by putting little bits of glass before your eyes. This is among the many magical beliefs that come from the conviction you are a body, and the body's eyes can see.

You also believe the body's brain can think. If you but understood the nature of thought, you could but laugh at this insane idea. It is as if you thought you held the match that lights the sun and gives it all its warmth; or that you held the world within your hand, securely bound until you let it go. Yet this is no more foolish than to believe the body's eyes can see; the brain can think.

D.U. ref.: 3. W159, *D.U.* page 228, *ACIM* location: W-PI.92.1.2–W-PI.92.2.4

Day 171

This course is a beginning, not an end. Your Friend goes with you.

D.U. ref.: 4. W487, *D.U.* page 228, *ACIM* location: W.ep.1

Day 172

This course remains within the ego framework, where it is needed.

D.U. ref.: 5. CL77, *D.U.* page 228, *ACIM* location: C-in.3.

Day 173

The sole responsibility of the miracle worker is to accept the Atonement for himself.

D.U. ref.: 6. T25–26, *D.U.* page 231, *ACIM* location: T-2.V.5.1

Day 174

I am not a body. I am free.
For I am still as God created me.

D.U. ref.: 7. W386, *D.U.* page 232, *ACIM* location: W-219.1.6

Day 175

The ego holds the body dear because it dwells in it, and lives united with the home that it has made. It is a part of the illusion that has sheltered it from being found illusory itself.

D.U. ref.: 8. W382, *D.U.* page 232, *ACIM* location: W-199.3.3

Day 176

As I have said before, "As you teach so shall you learn."

D.U. ref.: 9. T82, *D.U.* page 232, *ACIM* location: T-6.I.6

Day 177

He who would not forgive must judge, for he must justify his failure to forgive.

D.U. ref.: 10. W401, D.U. page 234, ACIM location: W-pII.1.4.4

Day 178

I do not call for martyrs but for teachers.

D.U. ref.: 11. T95, D.U. page 234, ACIM location: T-6.I.16.3

Day 179

A tranquil mind is not a little gift.

D.U. ref.: 12. M51, D.U. page 235, ACIM location: M-20.4.8

Day 180

The miracle establishes you dream a dream, and that its content is not true. This is a crucial step in dealing with illusions. No one is afraid of them when he perceives he made them up. The fear was held in place because he did not see that he was author of the dream, and not a figure in the dream.

D.U. ref.: 13. T594, D.U. page 236, ACIM location: T-28.II.7

Day 181

The miracle is the first step in giving back to cause the function of causation, not effect.

D.U. ref.: 14. T595, *D.U.* page 236, *ACIM* location: T-28.II.9.3

Day 182

Join not your brother's dreams but join with him, and where you join His Son the Father is.

D.U. ref.: 15. T600, *D.U.* page 237, *ACIM* location: T-28.IV.10

Day 183

You share no evil dreams if you forgive the dreamer, and perceive that he is not the dream he made. And so he cannot be a part of yours, from which you both are free.

D.U. ref.: 16. T601, *D.U.* page 237, *ACIM* location: T-28.V.3

Day 184

Prisoners bound with heavy chains for years, starved and emaciated, weak and exhausted, and with eyes so long cast down in darkness they remember not the light, do not leap up in joy the instant they are made free. It takes a while for them to understand what freedom is.

D.U. ref.: 17. T431, *D.U.* page 237, *ACIM* location: T-20.III.9

Day 185

There is a very simple way to find the door to true forgiveness, and perceive it open wide in welcome. When you feel that you are tempted to accuse someone of sin in any form, do not allow your mind to dwell on what you think he did, for that is self-deception. Ask instead, "Would I accuse myself of doing this?"

D.U. ref.: 18. W249, *D.U.* page 238, *ACIM* location: W-134.9

Day 186

The ability to accept truth in this world is the perceptual counterpart of creating in the Kingdom. God will do His part if you will do yours, and His return in exchange for yours is the exchange of knowledge for perception.

D.U. ref.: 19. T183, *D.U.* page 239, *ACIM* location: T-10.II.3.3

Day 187

The Holy Spirit is in both your minds, and He is One because there is no gap that separates His Oneness from Itself. The gap between your bodies matters not, for what is joined in Him is always one.

D.U. ref.: 20. T599, *D.U.* page 240, *ACIM* location: T-28.IV.7

Day 188

This change requires, first, that the cause be identified and then let go, so that it can be replaced.

D.U. ref.: 21. W34, *D.U.* page 240, *ACIM* location: W-23.5.2

Day 189

The first two steps in this process require your cooperation. The final one does not. Your images have already been replaced. By taking the first two steps, you will see that this is so.

D.U. ref.: 22. Ibid, *D.U.* page 240, *ACIM* location: W-23.5.6

Day 190

There is no order of difficulty in miracles. One is not "harder" or "bigger" than another. They are all the same. All expressions of love are maximal.

D.U. ref.: 23. T3, *D.U.* page 241, *ACIM* location: T-1.I.1

Day 191

Why wait for Heaven? Those who seek the light are merely covering their eyes. The light is in them now.

D.U. ref.: 24. W357, *D.U.* page 244, *ACIM* location: W-188.1

Day 192

To say these words is nothing. But to mean these words is everything.

D.U. ref.: 25. W348, *D.U.* page 245, *ACIM* location: W-185.1

Day 193

To mean you want the peace of God is to renounce all dreams.

D.U. ref.: 26. Ibid, *D.U.* page 245, *ACIM* location: W-185.5

Day 194

Fear binds the world. Forgiveness sets it free.

D.U. ref.: 27. W468, *D.U.* page 245, *ACIM* location: W-32-Title

Day 195

Assault can ultimately be made only on the body. There is little doubt that one body can assault another, and can even destroy it. Yet if destruction itself is impossible, anything that is destructible cannot be real. Its destruction, therefore, does not justify anger. To the extent to which you believe that it does, you are accepting false premises and teaching them to others. The message the crucifixion was intended to teach was that it is not necessary to perceive any form of assault in persecution, because you cannot *be* persecuted. If you respond with anger, you must be equating yourself with the destructible, and are therefore regarding yourself insanely.

D.U. ref.: 28. T92, *D.U.* page 246, *ACIM* location: T-6.I.4

Day 196

The message of the crucifixion is perfectly clear: *Teach only love, for that is what you are.*

If you interpret the crucifixion in any other way, you are using it as a weapon for assault rather than as the call for peace for which it was intended.

D.U. ref.: 29. T94, *D.U.* page 247, *ACIM* location:
T-6.I.13–T-6.I.14

Day 197

You choose your dreams, for they are what you wish, perceived as if it had been given you. Your idols do what you would have them do, and have the power you ascribe to them. And you pursue them vainly in the dream, because you want their power as your own.

Yet where are dreams but in a mind asleep? And can a dream succeed in making real the picture it projects outside itself? Save time, my brother; learn what time is for.

D.U. ref.: 30. T618–619, *D.U.* page 249, *ACIM* location:
T-29.VII.8.4–T-29.VII.9

Day 198

And each unfairness that the world appears to lay upon you, you have laid on it by rendering it purposeless, without the function that the Holy Spirit sees. And simple justice has been thus denied to every living thing upon the earth.

What this injustice does to you who judge unfairly, and who see as you have judged, you cannot calculate. The world grows dim and threatening, not a trace of all the happy sparkle that salvation brings can you perceive to lighten up your way. And so you see yourself deprived of light, abandoned to the dark, unfairly left without a purpose in a futile world. The world is fair because the Holy Spirit has brought injustice to the light within, and there has all unfairness been resolved and been replaced with justice and with love.

D.U. ref.: 31. T564, *D.U.* page 252, *ACIM* location: T-26.X.5.7–T-26.X.6.4

Day 199

To give this gift is how to make it yours.

D.U. ref.: 32. T668, *D.U.* page 253, *ACIM* location: T-31.VIII.8.6

Day 200

A miracle is never lost. It may touch many people you have not even met, and produce undreamed of changes in situations of which you are not even aware.

D.U. ref.: 33. T6, *D.U.* page 253, *ACIM* location: T-1.I.45

Day 201

And now he must attain a state that may remain impossible to reach for a long, long time. He must learn to lay all judgment aside, and ask only what he really wants in every circumstance.

D.U. ref.: 34. M11, *D.U.* page 255, *ACIM* location: M-4.I.A.7.7

Day 202

And finally, there is "a period of achievement." It is here that learning is consolidated. Now what was seen as merely shadows before become solid gains, to be counted on in all "emergencies" as well as tranquil times. Indeed, the tranquility is their result; the outcome of honest learning, consistency of thought and full transfer. This is the stage of real peace, for here is Heaven's state fully reflected.

D.U. ref.: 35. Ibid, *D.U.* page 255, *ACIM* location: M-4.I.A.8

Day 203

Be vigilant only for God and His Kingdom.

D.U. ref.: 36. T109, *D.U.* page 256, *ACIM* location: T-6.V.2.8

Day 204

Miracles arise from a miraculous state of mind, or a state of miracle-readiness.

D.U. ref.: 37. T6, *D.U.* page 256, *ACIM* location: T-1.I.43

Day 205

And thus will all the vestiges of hell, the secret sins and hidden hates be gone. And all the loveliness which they concealed appear like lawns of Heaven to our sight, to lift us high above the thorny roads we traveled on before the Christ appeared.

D.U. ref.: 38. T668, *D.U.* page 257, *ACIM* location: T-31.VIII.9.2

CHAPTER 12

About Enlightenment

Day 206

Enlightenment is but a recognition, not a change at all.

D.U. ref.: 1. W357, *D.U.* page 259, *ACIM* location: W-188.1.4

Day 207

Forgiveness recognizes what you thought your brother did to you has not occurred. It does not pardon sins and make them real. It sees there was no sin. And in that view are all your sins forgiven.

D.U. ref.: 2. W401, *D.U.* page 260, *ACIM* location: W-pII.1.1

Day 208

Minds are joined; bodies are not. Only by assigning to the mind the properties of the body does separation seem to be possible.

D.U. ref.: 3. T385, *D.U.* page 262, *ACIM* location: T-18.VI.3

Day 209

Your other life has continued without interruption, and has been and always will be totally unaffected by your attempts to dissociate it.

D.U. ref.: 4. T67, *D.U.* page 262, *ACIM* location: T-4.VI.1.7

Day 210

Salvation is for the mind, and it is attained through peace. This is the only thing that can be saved and the only way to save it.

D.U. ref.: 5. T221, *D.U.* page 264, *ACIM* location: T-12.III.5

Day 211

And what they hid is now revealed; an altar to the holy Name of God whereon His Word is written, with the gifts of your forgiveness laid before it, and the memory of God not far behind.

D.U. ref.: 6. W407, *D.U.* page 265, *ACIM* location: W-pII.2.3.4

Day 212

Your resurrection is your reawakening.

D.U. ref.: 7. T93, *D.U.* page 265, *ACIM* location: T-6.I.7

Day 213

Now you must learn that only infinite patience produces immediate effects.

D.U. ref.: 8. T88, *D.U.* page 265, *ACIM* location: T-5.VI.12

Day 214

Revelation induces complete but temporary suspension of doubt and fear. It reflects the original form of communication between God and His creations, involving the extremely personal sense of creation sometimes sought in physical relationships.

D.U. ref.: 9. T7, *D.U.* page 265, *ACIM* location: T-1.II.1

Day 215

We say "God is," and then we cease to speak, for in that knowledge words are meaningless. There are no lips to speak them, and no part of mind sufficiently distinct to feel that it is now aware of something not itself. It has united with its Source. And like its Source Itself, it merely is.

D.U. ref.: 10. W323, D.U. page 266, ACIM location: W-169.5.4

Day 216

The real world is the symbol that the dream of sin and guilt is over, and God's Son no longer sleeps. His waking eyes perceive the sure reflection of his Father's Love; the certain promise that he is redeemed. The real world signifies the end of time, for its perception makes time purposeless.

D.U. ref.: 11. W443, D.U. page 267, ACIM location: W-pII.8.4

Day 217

A universal theology is impossible, but a universal experience is not only possible but necessary. It is this experience toward which the course is directed.

D.U. ref.: 12. CL77, D.U. page 267, ACIM location: C-in.2.5

Day 218

When you unite with me you are uniting without the ego, because I have renounced the ego in myself and therefore cannot unite with yours. Our union is therefore the way to renounce the ego in you.

D.U. ref.: 13. T147, *D.U.* page 268, *ACIM* location: T-8.V.4

Day 219

Salvation is a paradox indeed! What could it be except a happy dream? It asks you but that you forgive all things that no one ever did; to overlook what is not there, and not to look upon the unreal as reality.

D.U. ref.: 14. T635, *D.U.* page 268, *ACIM* location: T-30.IV.7

Day 220

So fearful is the dream, so seeming real, he could not waken to reality without the sweat of terror and a scream of mortal fear, unless a gentler dream preceded his awaking, and allowed his calmer mind to welcome, not to fear, the Voice that calls with love to waken him; a gentler dream, in which his suffering was healed and where his brother was his friend.

D.U. ref.: 15. T584, *D.U.* pages 268–269, *ACIM* location: T-27.VII.13.4

Day 221

Can you to whom God says, "Release My Son!" be tempted not to listen, when you learn that it is you for whom He asks release?

D.U. ref.: 16. T666, *D.U.* page 269, *ACIM* location: T-31.VII.15.5

Day 222

Very simply, the resurrection is the overcoming or surmounting of death. It is a reawakening or a rebirth; a change of mind about the meaning of the world.

D.U. ref.: 17. M68, *D.U.* page 269, *ACIM* location: M-28.1

Day 223

The resurrection is the denial of death, being the assertion of life. Thus is all the thinking of the world reversed entirely.

D.U. ref.: 18. Ibid, *D.U.* page 269, *ACIM* location: M-28.2

Day 224

Christ's face is seen in every living thing, and nothing is held in darkness, apart from the light of forgiveness.

D.U. ref.: 19. Ibid, *D.U.* page 269, *ACIM* location: M-28.2.6

Day 225

Here the curriculum ends. From here on, no directions are needed. Vision is wholly corrected and all mistakes undone. Attack is meaningless and peace has come. The goal of the curriculum has been achieved. Thoughts turn to Heaven and away from hell. All longings are satisfied, for what remains unanswered or incomplete?

D.U. ref.: 20. Ibid, *D.U.* page 270, *ACIM* location: M-28.3

Day 226

The Second Coming is the one event in time which time itself can not affect. For every one who ever came to die, or yet will come or who is present now, is equally released from what he made. In this equality is Christ restored as one Identity, in which the Sons of God acknowledge that they all are one. And God the Father smiles upon His Son, His one creation and His only joy.

D.U. ref.: 21. W449, *D.U.* page 270, *ACIM* location: W-pII.9.4

Day 227

This is God's Final Judgment: "You are still My holy Son, forever innocent, forever loving and forever loved, as limitless as your Creator, and completely changeless and forever pure. Therefore awaken and return to Me. I am your Father and you are My Son."

D.U. ref.: 22. W455, *D.U.* page 270, *ACIM* location: W-pII.10.5

Day 228

When you perceive yourself without deceit, you will accept the real world in place of the false one you have made. And then your Father will lean down to you and take the last step for you, by raising you unto Himself.

D.U. ref.: 23. T214, *D.U.* page 271, *ACIM* location: T-11.VIII.15.4

Day 229

Heaven is not a place nor a condition. It is merely an awareness of perfect Oneness, and the knowledge that there is nothing else; nothing outside this Oneness, and nothing else within.

D.U. ref.: 24. T384, *D.U.* page 272, *ACIM* location: T-18.VI.1.5

Day 230

There are no beginnings and no endings in God, Whose universe is Himself.

D.U. ref.: 25. T194, *D.U.* page 272, *ACIM* location: T-11.I.2.3

Day 231

The universe of love does not stop because you do not see it, nor have your closed eyes lost the ability to see.

D.U. ref.: 26. T195, *D.U.* page 272, *ACIM* location: T-11.I.5.10

Day 232

God has given you a place in His Mind that is yours forever. Yet you can keep it only by giving it, as it was given you.

D.U. ref.: 27. Ibid, *D.U.* page 272, *ACIM* location: T-11.I.6

Day 233

God is, and in Him all created things must be eternal. Do you not see that otherwise He has an opposite, and fear would be as real as love?

D.U. ref.: 28. M67, *D.U.* page 273, *ACIM* location: M-27.6.10

Day 234

Oneness is simply the idea God is. And in His Being, He encompasses all things. No mind holds anything but Him.

D.U. ref.: 29. W323, *D.U.* page 273, *ACIM* location: W-169.5

CHAPTER 13

About Out-of-Body Experiences

Day 235

The universe is waiting your release because it is its own.

D.U. ref.: 1. S22, *D.U.* page 275, *ACIM* location: S-3.IV.10.3

Day 236

It would indeed be strange if you were asked to go beyond all symbols of the world, forgetting them forever; yet were asked to take a teaching function. You have need to use the symbols of the world a while. But be you not deceived by them as well. They do not stand for anything at all, and in your practicing it is this thought that will release you from them.

D.U. ref.: 2. W346, *D.U.* page 276, *ACIM* location: W-184.9

Day 237

Thus what you need are intervals each day in which the learning of the world becomes a transitory phase; a prison house from which you go into the sunlight and forget the darkness. Here you understand the Word, the Name which God has given you; the one Identity which all things share; the one acknowledgment of what is true. And then step back to darkness, not because you think it real, but only to proclaim its unreality in terms which still have meaning in the world that darkness rules.

D.U. ref.: 3. Ibid, *D.U.* page 276, *ACIM* location: W-184.10

Day 238

You cannot cancel out your past errors alone. They will not disappear from your mind without the Atonement, a remedy not of your making.

D.U. ref.: 4. T81, *D.U.* page 277, *ACIM* location: T-5.IV.2.9

Day 239

You might put it this way: *My salvation comes from me. It cannot come from anywhere else.*

D.U. ref.: 5. W119, *D.U.* page 277, *ACIM* location: W-70.7.3

Day 240

What has been given you? The knowledge that you are a mind, in Mind and purely mind, sinless forever, wholly unafraid, because you were created out of love. Nor have you left your Source, remaining as you were created.

D.U. ref.: 6. W298, *D.U.* page 277, *ACIM* location: W-158.1

Day 241

There is a way of living in the world that is not here, although it seems to be. You do not change appearance, though you smile more frequently. Your forehead is serene; your eyes are quiet.

D.U. ref.: 7. W291, *D.U.* page 278, *ACIM* location: W-155.1

Day 242

You walk this path as others walk, nor do you seem to be distinct from them, although you are indeed. Thus can you serve them while you serve yourself, and set their footsteps on the way that God has opened up to you, and them through you.

D.U. ref.: 8. Ibid, *D.U.* page 278, *ACIM* location: W-155.5.3

Day 243

Christ's hand has touched your shoulder, and you feel that you are not alone.

D.U. ref.: 9. W316, *D.U.* page 279, *ACIM* location: W-166.9.2

Day 244

As the ego would limit your perception of your brothers to the body, so would the Holy Spirit release your vision and let you see the Great Rays shining from them, so unlimited that they reach to God.

D.U. ref.: 10. T322, *D.U.* page 279, *ACIM* location: T-15.IX.1

Day 245

Revelation unites you directly with God.

D.U. ref.: 11. T7, *D.U.* page 281, *ACIM* location: T-1.II.1.5

Day 246

Revelation is not reciprocal. It proceeds from God to you, but not from you to God.

D.U. ref.: 12. T8, *D.U.* page 281, *ACIM* location: T-1.II.5.4

Day 247

Awe should be reserved for revelation, to which it is perfectly and correctly applicable.

D.U. ref.: 13. T7, *D.U.* page 281, *ACIM* location: T-1.II.3

Day 248

Revelation is literally unspeakable because it is an experience of unspeakable love.

D.U. ref.: 14. Ibid, *D.U.* page 282, *ACIM* location: T-1.II.2.7

Day 249

No one who has experienced the revelation of this can ever fully believe in the ego again.

D.U. ref.: 15. T60–61, *D.U.* page 282, *ACIM* location: T-4.III.3.7

Day 250

Healing is of God in the end. The means are being carefully explained to you. Revelation may occasionally reveal the end to you, but to reach it the means are needed.

D.U. ref.: 16. T16, *D.U.* page 282, *ACIM* location: T-1.VII.5.9

Day 251

Revelation induces complete but temporary suspension of doubt and fear.

D.U. ref.: 17. T7, *D.U.* page 282, *ACIM* location: T-1.II.1

Day 252

Certainly there are many "psychic" powers that are clearly in line with this course.

D.U. ref.: 18. M62, *D.U.* page 284, *ACIM* location: M-25.2

Day 253

The limits the world places on communication are the chief barriers to direct experience of the Holy Spirit.

D.U. ref.: 19. Ibid , *D.U.* page 284, *ACIM* location: M-25.2.5

Day 254

Who transcends these limits in any way is merely becoming more natural.

D.U. ref.: 20. Ibid, *D.U.* page 284, *ACIM* location: M-25.2.7

Day 255

God gives no special favors, and no one has any powers that are not available to everyone.

D.U. ref.: 21. Ibid, *D.U.* page 284, *ACIM* location: M-25.3.7

Day 256

Nothing that is genuine is used to deceive.

D.U. ref.: 22. Ibid, *D.U.* page 284, *ACIM* location: M-25.4

Day 257

As his awareness increases, he may well develop abilities that seem quite startling to him. Yet nothing he can do can compare even in the slightest with the glorious surprise of remembering Who he is. Let all his learning and all his efforts be directed toward this one great final surprise, and he will not be content to be delayed by the little ones that may come to him on the way.

D.U. ref.: 23. Ibid, *D.U.* page 284, *ACIM* location: M-25.1.4

Day 258

As you read the teachings of the Apostles, remember that I told them myself that there was much they would understand later, because they were not wholly ready to follow me at the time.

D.U. ref.: 24. T95, *D.U.* pages 293–294, *ACIM* location: T-6.I.16

Day 259

It is in your power to make this season holy, for it is in your power to make the time of Christ be now. It is possible to do this all at once because there is but one shift in perception that is necessary, for you made but one mistake.

D.U. ref.: 25. T325, *D.U.* page 298, *ACIM* location: T-15.X.4

Day 260

This world you seem to live in is not home to you. And somewhere in your mind you know that this is true.

D.U. ref.: 26. W339, *D.U.* page 298, *ACIM* location: W-182.1

Day 261

God loves His Son. Request Him now to give the means by which this world will disappear, and vision first will come, with knowledge but an instant later.

D.U. ref.: 27. W321, *D.U.* page 298, *ACIM* location: W-168.4

Day 262

Make this year different by making it all the same.

D.U. ref.: 28. T329, *D.U.* page 298, *ACIM* location: T-15.XI.10.11

Day 263

Now is he redeemed. And as he sees the gates of Heaven stand open before him, he will enter in and disappear into the Heart of God.

D.U. ref.: 29. W479, *D.U.* page 298, *ACIM* location: W-pII.14.5.4

CHAPTER 14

About Healing the Sick

Day 264

The acceptance of sickness as a decision of the mind, for a purpose for which it would use the body, is the basis of healing. And this is so for healing in all forms.

D.U. ref.: 1. M18, *D.U.* page 299, *ACIM* location: M-5.II.2

Day 265

You travel but in dreams, while safe at home.

D.U. ref.: 2. T257, *D.U.* page 300, *ACIM* location: T-13.VII.17.7

Day 266

Choose once again what you would have [the Son of God] be, remembering that every choice you make establishes your own identity as you will see it and believe it is.

D.U. ref.: 3. T667, *D.U.* page 302, *ACIM* location: T-31.VIII.6.5

Day 267

The process that takes place in this relationship is actually one in which the therapist in his heart tells the patient that all his sins have been forgiven him, along with his own. What could be the difference between healing and forgiveness?

D.U. ref.: 4. P17, *D.U.* page 302, *ACIM* location: P-2.VII.3

Day 268

There is a way in which escape is possible. It can be learned and taught, but it requires patience and abundant willingness.

D.U. ref.: 5. M46, *D.U.* page 304, *ACIM* location: M-17.8.3

Day 269

What is the single requisite for this shift in perception? It is simply this; the recognition that sickness is of the mind, and has nothing to do with the body. What does this recognition "cost"? It costs the whole world you see, for the world will never again appear to rule the mind.

D.U. ref.: 6. M18, *D.U.* page 305, *ACIM* location: M-5.II.3

Day 270

Who is the physician? Only the mind of the patient himself. The outcome is what he decides that it is. Special agents seem to be ministering to him, yet they but give form to his own choice. He chooses them in order to bring tangible form to his desires.

D.U. ref.: 7. Ibid, *D.U.* page 306, *ACIM* location: M-5.II.2.5

Day 271

The world does nothing to him. He only thought it did. Nor does he do anything to the world, because he was mistaken about what it is. Herein is the release from guilt and sickness both, for they are one.

D.U. ref.: 8. Ibid, *D.U.* page 306, *ACIM* location: M-5.II.3.8

Day 272

What you behold as sickness and as pain, as weakness and as suffering and loss, is but temptation to perceive yourself defenseless and in hell.

D.U. ref.: 9. T667, *D.U.* page 306, *ACIM* location: T-31.VIII.6.2

Day 273

A miracle has come to heal God's Son, and close the door upon his dreams of weakness, opening the way to his salvation and release.

D.U. ref.: 10. Ibid, *D.U.* page 306, *ACIM* location: T-31.VIII.6.4

Day 274

And thus are miracles as natural as fear and agony appeared to be before the choice for holiness was made. For in that choice are false distinctions gone, illusory alternatives laid by, and nothing left to interfere with truth.

D.U. ref.: 11. Ibid, *D.U.* page 307, *ACIM* location: T-31.VIII.5.6

Day 275

To them God's teachers come, to represent another choice which they had forgotten. The simple presence of a teacher of God is a reminder.

D.U. ref.: 12. M19, *D.U.* page 307, *ACIM* location: M-5.III.2

Day 276

Very gently they call to their brothers to turn away from death: "Behold, you Son of God, what life can offer you. Would you choose sickness in place of this?"

D.U. ref.: 13. Ibid, *D.U.* page 307, *ACIM* location: M-5.III.2.11

Day 277

When all magic is recognized as merely nothing, the teacher of God has reached the most advanced state.

D.U. ref.: 14. M42, *D.U.* page 308, *ACIM* location: M-16.9.5

Day 278

Only salvation can be said to cure.

D.U. ref.: 15. 270, *D.U.* page 309, *ACIM* location: W-140.12.2

Day 279

Atonement does not heal the sick, for that is not a cure. It takes away the guilt that makes the sickness possible. And that is cure indeed.

D.U. ref.: 16. Ibid, *D.U.* page 309, *ACIM* location: W-140.4.4

Day 280

Being sane, the mind heals the body because it has been healed. The sane mind cannot conceive of illness because it cannot conceive of attacking anyone or anything.

D.U. ref.: 17. T84, *D.U.* page 309, *ACIM* location: T-5.V.5.2

Day 281

The ego believes that by punishing itself it will mitigate the punishment of God. Yet even in this it is arrogant. It attributes to God a punishing intent, and then takes this intent as its own prerogative.

D.U. ref.: 18. T84–85, *D.U.* page 309, *ACIM* location: T-5.V.5.6

Day 282

Your minds are not separate, and God has only one channel for healing because He has but one Son. God's remaining Communication Link with all His children joins them together, and them to Him.

D.U. ref.: 19. T184, *D.U.* page 309, *ACIM* location: T-10.III.2.5

Day 283

It is not the function of God's teachers to evaluate the outcome of their gifts. It is merely their function to give them.

D.U. ref.: 20. M20, *D.U.* page 313, *ACIM* location: M-6.3

CHAPTER 15

About Time

Day 284

Time lasted but an instant in your mind, with no effect upon eternity. And so is all time past, and everything exactly as it was before the way to nothingness was made. The tiny tick of time in which the first mistake was made, and all of them within that one mistake, held also the Correction for that one, and all of them that came within the first. And in that tiny instant time was gone, for that was all it ever was.

D.U. ref.: 1. T550, *D.U.* page 315, *ACIM* location: T-26.V.3.3

Day 285

I am as God created me. His Son can suffer nothing. And I am His Son.

D.U. ref.: 2. T667, *D.U.* page 316, *ACIM* location: T-31.VIII.5.2

Day 286

Ultimately, space is as meaningless as time. Both are merely beliefs.

D.U. ref.: 3. T14, *D.U.* page 317, *ACIM* location: T-1.VI.3.5

Day 287

What seems to be the opposite of life is merely sleeping. When the mind elects to be what it is not, and to assume an alien power which it does not have, a foreign state it cannot enter, or a false condition not within its Source, it merely seems to go to sleep a while.

D.U. ref.: 4. W319, *D.U.* page 317, *ACIM* location: W-167.9

Day 288

It dreams of time; an interval in which what seems to happen never has occurred, the changes wrought are substanceless, and all events are nowhere. When the mind awakes, it but continues as it always was.

D.U. ref.: 5. Ibid, *D.U.* page 318, *ACIM* location: W-167.9.3

Day 289

Each day, and every minute in each day, and every instant that each minute holds, you but relive the single instant when the time of terror took the place of love. And so you die each day to live again, until you cross the gap between the past and present, which is not a gap at all. Such is each life; a seeming interval from birth to death and on to life again, a repetition of an instant gone by long ago that cannot be relived. And all of time is but the mad belief that what is over is still here and now.

Forgive the past and let it go, for it is gone.

D.U. ref.: 6. T552, *D.U.* page 318, *ACIM* location: T-26.V.13–T-26.V.14

Day 290

Behold the great projection, but look on it with the decision that it must be healed, and not with fear. Nothing you made has any power over you unless you still would be apart from your Creator, and with a will opposed to His.

D.U. ref.: 7. T473, *D.U.* page 319, *ACIM* location: T-22.II.10

Day 291

For time you made, and time you can command. You are no more a slave to time than to the world you made.

D.U. ref.: 8. Ibid, *D.U.* page 319, *ACIM* location: T-22.II.8.7

Day 292

There is no part of Heaven you can take and weave into illusions. Nor is there one illusion you can enter Heaven with.

D.U. ref.: 9. Ibid, *D.U.* page 319, *ACIM* location: T-22.II.8

Day 293

The revelation that the Father and the Son are one will come in time to every mind. Yet is that time determined by the mind itself, not taught.

The time is set already. It appears to be quite arbitrary. Yet there is no step along the road that anyone takes but by chance. It has already been taken by him, although he has not yet embarked on it. For time but seems to go in one direction. We but undertake a journey that is over. Yet it seems to have a future still unknown to us.

Time is a trick, a sleight of hand, a vast illusion in which figures come and go as if by magic. Yet there is a plan behind appearances that does not change. The script is written. When experience will come to end your doubting has been set. For we but see the journey from the point at which it ended, looking back on it, imagining we make it once again; reviewing mentally what has gone by.

D.U. ref.: 10. W298, *D.U.* page 320, *ACIM* location:
W-158.2.8–W-158.4.5

Day 294

[Time] returns the mind into the endless present, where the past and future cannot be conceived.

D.U. ref.: 11. W323–324, *D.U.* page 321, *ACIM* location: W-169.6.3

Day 295

The world has never been at all. Eternity remains a constant state.

D.U. ref.: 12. W324, *D.U.* page 321, *ACIM* location: W-169.6.6

Day 296

This is beyond experience we try to hasten. Yet forgiveness, taught and learned, brings with it the experiences which bear witness that the time the mind itself determined to abandon all but this is now at hand.

D.U. ref.: 13. T153, *D.U.* page 321, *ACIM* location: W-169.7

Day 297

All learning was already in His Mind, accomplished and complete. He recognized all that time holds, and gave it to all minds that each one might determine, from a point where time was ended, when it is released to revelation and eternity. We have repeated several times before that you but make a journey that is done.

For oneness must be here. Whatever time the mind has set for revelation is entirely irrelevant to what must be a constant state, forever as it always was; forever to remain as it is now.

D.U. ref.: 14. Ibid, *D.U.* page 321, *ACIM* location: W-169.8–W-169.9.2

Day 298

Suffice it, then, that you have work to do to play your part. The ending must remain obscure to you until your part is done. It does not matter. For your part is still what all the rest depends on. As you take the role assigned to you, salvation comes a little nearer each uncertain heart that does not beat as yet in tune with God.

D.U. ref.: 15. Ibid, *D.U.* page 322, *ACIM* location: W-169.11

Day 299

Forgiveness is the central theme that runs throughout salvation, holding all its parts in meaningful relationships, the course it runs directed and its outcome sure.

D.U. ref.: 16. Ibid, *D.U.* page 322, *ACIM* location: W-169.12

Day 300

Choose once again if you would take your place among the saviors of the world, or would remain in hell, and hold your brothers there.

D.U. ref.: 17. T666, *D.U.* page 322, *ACIM* location: T-31.VIII.1.5

Day 301

Your brothers are everywhere. You do not have to seek far for salvation. Every minute and every second gives you a chance to save yourself. Do not lose these chances, not because they will not return, but because delay of joy is needless.

D.U. ref.: 18. T175, *D.U.* page 324, *ACIM* location: T-9.VII.1.5

Day 302

You are much too tolerant of mind wandering, and are passively condoning your mind's miscreations.

D.U. ref.: 19. T29, *D.U.* page 325, *ACIM* location: T-2.VI.4.6

Day 303

There is a borderland of thought that stands between this world and Heaven. It is not a place, and when you reach it is apart from time. Here is the meeting place where thoughts are brought together; where conflicting values meet and all illusions are laid down beside the truth, where they are judged to be untrue. This borderland is just beyond the gate of Heaven. Here is every thought made pure and wholly simple. Here is sin denied, and everything that is received instead.

D.U. ref.: 20. T546, *D.U.* page 329, *ACIM* location: T-26.III.2

Day 304

This is the journey's end. We have referred to it as the real world.

D.U. ref.: 21. T547, *D.U.* page 329, *ACIM* location: T-26.III.3

Day 305

The Holy Spirit must perceive time, and reinterpret it into the timeless. He must work through opposites, because He must work with and for a mind that is in opposition. Correct and learn, and be open to learning. You have not made truth, but truth can still set you free.

D.U. ref.: 22. T80, *D.U.* page 329, *ACIM* location: T-5.III.11.2

Day 306

In time the giving comes first, though they are simultaneous in eternity, where they cannot be separated. When you have learned they are the same, the need for time is over.

Eternity is one time, its only dimension being "always."

D.U. ref.: 23. T174–175, *D.U.* page 330, *ACIM* location: T-9.VI.6.4–T-9.VI.7

Day 307

Time and eternity are both in your mind, and will conflict until you perceive time solely as a means to regain eternity.

D.U. ref.: 24. T181, *D.U.* page 330, *ACIM* location: T-10.in.1.2

Day 308

Can you find light by analyzing darkness, as the psychotherapist does, or like the theologian, by acknowledging darkness in yourself and looking for a distant light to remove it, while emphasizing the distance?

D.U. ref.: 25. T172, *D.U.* page 330, *ACIM* location: T-9.V.6.3

Day 309

And where is time, when dreams of judgment have been put away?

D.U. ref.: 26. T624, *D.U.* page 332, *ACIM* location: T-29.IX.8.6

CHAPTER 16

About Watching Worldly Events Unfold

Day 310

You cannot see his sins and not your own. But you can free him and yourself as well.

D.U. ref.: 1. S10, *D.U.* page 333, *ACIM* location: S-2.I.5.7

Day 311

By far the majority are given a slowly evolving training program, in which as many previous mistakes as possible are corrected. Relationships in particular must be properly perceived, and all dark cornerstones of unforgiveness removed. Otherwise the old thought system still has a basis for return.

D.U. ref.: 2. M26, *D.U.* page 335, *ACIM* location: M-9.1.7

Day 312

This course is always practical. It may be that the teacher of God is not in a situation that fosters quiet thought as he awakes. If this is so, let him but remember that he chooses to spend time with God as soon as possible, and let him do so.

D.U. ref.: 3. M40–41, *D.U.* page 335, *ACIM* location: M-16.4.1

Day 313

On the contrary, he puts himself in a position where judgment *through* him rather than by him can occur. And this judgment is neither "good" nor "bad." It is the only judgment there is, and it is only one: "God's Son is guiltless, and sin does not exist."

D.U. ref.: 4. M27, *D.U.* page 336, *ACIM* location: M-10.2.7

Day 314

Preoccupations with problems set up to be incapable of solution are favorite ego devices for impeding learning progress. In all these diversionary tactics, however, the one question that is never asked by those who pursue them is, "What for?" This is the question that you must learn to ask in connection with everything. What is the purpose? Whatever it is, it will direct your efforts automatically.

D.U. ref.: 5. T67, *D.U.* page 340, *ACIM* location: T-4.V.6.6

Day 315

Is it a sacrifice to give up pain? Does an adult resent the giving up of children's toys? Does one whose vision has already glimpsed the face of Christ look back with longing on a slaughter house? No one who has escaped the world and all its ills looks back on it with condemnation. Yet he must rejoice that he is free of all the sacrifice its values would demand of him.

D.U. ref.: 6. M33, *D.U.* page 343, *ACIM* location: M-13.4.2

Day 316

Have faith in only this one thing, and it will be sufficient: God wills you be in Heaven, and nothing can keep you from it, or it from you. Your wildest misperceptions, your weird imaginings, your blackest nightmares all mean nothing. They will not prevail against the peace God wills for you.

D.U. ref.: 7. T268, *D.U.* page 344, *ACIM* location: T-13.XI.7

CHAPTER 17

About True Prayer and Abundance

Day 317

I once asked you to sell all you have and give to the poor and follow me. This is what I meant: If you have no investment in anything in this world, you can teach the poor where their treasure is. The poor are merely those who have invested wrongly, and they are poor indeed!

D.U. ref.: 1. T220, D.U. page 345, ACIM location: T-12.III

Day 318

The secret of true prayer is to forget the things you think you need. To ask for the specific is much the same as to look on sin and then forgive it. Also in the same way, in prayer you overlook your specific needs as you see them, and let them go into God's Hands. There they become your gifts to Him, for they tell Him that you would have no gods before Him; no Love but His.

D.U. ref.: 2. S2, D.U. page 351, ACIM location: S-1.I.4

Day 319

The form of the answer, if given by God, will suit your need as you see it. This is merely an echo of the reply of His Voice. The real sound is always a song of thanksgiving and of Love.

D.U. ref.: 3. Ibid, *D.U.* page 352, *ACIM* location: S-1.I.2.7

Day 320

You cannot, then, ask for the echo. It is the song that is the gift. Along with it come the overtones, the harmonics, the echoes, but these are secondary.

D.U. ref.: 4. Ibid, *D.U.* page 352, *ACIM* location: S-1.I.3

Day 321

God answers only for eternity. But still all little answers are contained in this.

D.U. ref.: 5. Ibid, *D.U.* page 353, *ACIM* location: S-1.I.4.7

Day 322

In true prayer you hear only the song. All the rest is merely added. You have sought first the Kingdom of Heaven, and all else has indeed been given you.

D.U. ref.: 6. Ibid, *D.U.* page 353, *ACIM* location: S-1.I.3.4

CHAPTER 18

About Revelation

Day 323

Revelation induces complete but temporary suspension of doubt and fear. It reflects the original form of communication between God and His creations, involving the extremely personal sense of creation sometimes sought in physical relationships. Physical closeness cannot achieve it.

D.U. ref.: 1. T7, *D.U.* page 355, *ACIM* location: T-1.II.1

Day 324

You are as God created you, and so is every living thing you look upon, regardless of the images you see. What you behold as sickness and as pain, as weakness and as suffering and loss, is but temptation to perceive yourself defenseless and in hell. Yield not to this, and you will see all pain, in every form, wherever it occurs, but disappear as mists before the sun. A miracle has come to heal God's Son, and close the door upon his dreams of weakness, opening the way to his salvation and release. Choose once again what you would have him be, remembering that every choice you make establishes your own identity as you will see it and believe it is.

D.U. ref.: 2. T667, *D.U.* page 356, *ACIM* location: T-31.VIII.6

Day 325

Fantasies are a means of making false associations and attempting to obtain pleasure from them. But although you can perceive false associations, you can never make them real except to yourself. You believe in what you make. If you offer miracles, you will be equally strong in your belief in them.

D.U. ref.: 3. T15, *D.U.* page 358, *ACIM* location: T-1.VII.3.6

Day 326

Let not their form deceive you. Idols are but substitutes for your reality. In some way, you believe they will complete your little self, for safety in a world perceived as dangerous, with forces massed against your confidence and peace of mind. They have the power to supply your lacks, and add the value that you do not have. No one believes in idols who has not enslaved himself to littleness and loss. And thus must seek beyond his little self for strength to raise his head, and stand apart from all the misery the world reflects. This is the penalty for looking not within for certainty and quiet calm that liberates you from the world, and lets you stand apart, in quiet and in peace.

D.U. ref.: 4. T619, *D.U.* page 358, *ACIM* location: T-29.VIII.2

Day 327

This course does not attempt to take from you the little that you have.

D.U. ref.: 5. W245, *D.U.* page 358, *ACIM* location: W-133.2.3

Day 328

Release the world! Your real creations wait for this release to give you fatherhood, not of illusions, but as God in truth. God shares His Fatherhood with you who are His Son, for He makes no distinctions in what is Himself and what is still Himself. What He creates is not apart from Him, and nowhere does the Father end, the Son begin as something separate from Him.

D.U. ref.: 6. W244, *D.U.* page 363, *ACIM* location: W-132.12

Day 329

Deny illusions, but accept the truth. Deny you are a shadow briefly laid upon a dying world. Release your mind, and you will look upon a world released.

D.U. ref.: 7. Ibid, *D.U.* page 364, *ACIM* location: W-132.13.4

Day 330

From the forgiven world the Son of God is lifted easily into his home. And there he knows that he has always rested there in peace. Even salvation will become a dream, and vanish from his mind. For salvation is the end of dreams, and with the closing of the dream will have no meaning. Who, awake in Heaven, could dream that there could ever be need of salvation?

D.U. ref.: 8. T354, *D.U.* page 365, *ACIM* location: T-17.II.7

CHAPTER 19

About the Future

Day 331

The presence of fear is a sure sign that you are trusting in your own strength.

D.U. ref.: 1. W77, *D.U.* page 367, *ACIM* location: W-48.3

Day 332

Can you to whom God says, "Release My Son!" be tempted not to listen, when you learn that it is you for whom He asks release?

D.U. ref.: 2. T666, *D.U.* page 369, *ACIM* location: T-31.VII.15.5

Day 333

Each worshipper of idols harbors hope his special deities will give him more than other men possess. It must be more. It does not really matter more of what; more beauty, more intelligence, more wealth, or even more affliction and more pain. But more of something is an idol for. And when one fails another takes its place, with hope of finding more of something else. Be not deceived by forms the "something" takes. An idol is a means for getting more. And it is this that is against God's Will.

God has not many Sons, but only One. Who can have more, and who be given less?

D.U. ref.: 3. T621, *D.U.* page 374, *ACIM* location:
T-29.VIII.8.7–T-29.VIII.9.2

Day 334

Salvation does not ask that you behold the spirit and perceive the body not. It merely asks that this should be your choice. For you can see the body without help, but do not understand how to behold a world apart from it. It is your world salvation will undo, and let you see another world your eyes could never find.

D.U. ref.: 4. T661, *D.U.* page 377, *ACIM* location: T-31.VI.3

Day 335

Seek not outside yourself. For it will fail, and you will weep each time an idol falls. Heaven cannot be found where it is not, and there can be no peace excepting there.

D.U. ref.: 5. T617, *D.U.* page 377, *ACIM* location: T-29.VII.1

Day 336

There is one major difference in the role of Heaven's messengers, which sets them off from those the world appoints. The messages that they deliver are intended first for them. And it is only as they can accept them for themselves that they become able to bring them further, and to give them everywhere that they were meant to be. Like earthly messengers, they did not write the messages they bear, but they become their first receivers in the truest sense, receiving to prepare themselves to give.

D.U. ref.: 6. W289, *D.U.* page 377, *ACIM* location: W-154.6

Day 337

To follow the Holy Spirit's guidance is to let yourself be absolved of guilt.

D.U. ref.: 7. M70, *D.U.* page 378, *ACIM* location: M-29.3.3

Day 338

Do not, then, think that following the Holy Spirit's guidance is necessary merely because of your own inadequacies. It is the way out of hell for you.

D.U. ref.: 8. Ibid, *D.U.* page 378, *ACIM* location: M-29.3.10

Day 339

Would God have left the meaning of the world to your interpretation?

D.U. ref.: 9. T640, *D.U.* page 378, *ACIM* location: T-30.VII.1

Day 340

Through you is ushered in a world unseen, unheard, yet truly there.

D.U. ref.: 10. M72, *D.U.* page 379, *ACIM* location: M-29.8.5

CHAPTER 20

About Raising the Dead

Day 341

Embodiment of fear, the host of sin, god of the guilty and the lord of all illusions and deceptions, does the thought of death seem mighty.

D.U. ref.: 1. W309, *D.U.* page 381, *ACIM* location: W-163.1

Day 342

And the last to be overcome will be death.

D.U. ref.: 2. M67, *D.U.* page 385, *ACIM* location: M-27.6.1

Day 343

And who could weep but for his innocence?

D.U. ref.: 3. P9, *D.U.* page 385, *ACIM* location: P-2.IV.1.7

Day 344

What is a miracle but this remembering? And who is there in whom this memory lies not?

D.U. ref.: 4. T447, *D.U.* page 386, *ACIM* location: T-21.I.10.4

Day 345

To you and your brother, in whose special relationship the Holy Spirit entered, it is given to release and be released from the dedication to death. For it was offered you, and you accepted. Yet you must learn still more about this strange devotion, for it contains the third obstacle that peace must flow across. No one can die unless he chooses death. What seems to be the fear of death is really its attraction.

D.U. ref.: 5. T416, *D.U.* page 386, *ACIM* location: T-19.IV.C.1

Day 346

All that must be recognized, however, is that birth was not the beginning, and death is not the end.

D.U. ref.: 6. M61, *D.U.* page 387, *ACIM* location: M-24.5.7

Day 347

Your mind will elect to join with mine, and together we are invincible. You and your brother will yet come together in my name, and your sanity will be restored. I raised the dead by knowing that life is an eternal attribute of everything that the living God created. Why do you believe it is harder for me to inspire the dis-spirited or to stabilize the unstable? I do not believe that there is an order of difficulty in miracles; you do.

D.U. ref.: 7. T65, *D.U.* page 388, *ACIM* location: T-4.IV.11.5

Day 348

If death is real for anything, there is no life. Death denies life. But if there is reality in life, death is denied. No compromise in this is possible. There is either a god of fear or One of Love. The world attempts a thousand compromises, and will attempt a thousand more. Not one can be acceptable to God's teachers, because not one could be acceptable to God. He did not make death because He did not make fear. Both are equally meaningless to Him.

The "reality" of death is firmly rooted in the belief that God's Son is a body. And if God created bodies, death would indeed be real. But God would not be loving. There is no point at which the contrast between the perception of the real world and that of the world of illusions becomes more sharply evident.

D.U. ref.: 8. M66–67, *D.U.* page 390, *ACIM* location:
M-27.4.2–M-27.5.4

Day 349

The real world is the symbol that the dream of sin and guilt is over, and God's Son no longer sleeps. His waking eyes perceive the sure reflection of his Father's Love; the certain promise that he is redeemed. The real world signifies the end of time, for its perception makes time purposeless.

D.U. ref.: 9. W443, *D.U.* page 390, *ACIM* location: W-PII.8.4

Day 350

In any state apart from Heaven life is illusion. At best it seems like life; at worst, like death. Yet both are judgments on what is not life, equal in their inaccuracy and lack of meaning. Life not in Heaven is impossible, and what is not in Heaven is not anywhere.

D.U. ref.: 10. T493–494, *D.U.* page 392, *ACIM* location: T-23.II.19.3

Day 351

The First Coming of Christ is merely another name for the creation, for Christ is the Son of God. The Second Coming of Christ means nothing more than the end of the ego's rule and the healing of the mind. I was created like you in the First, and I have called you to join with me in the Second.

D.U. ref.: 11. T64, *D.U.* page 392, *ACIM* location: T-4.IV.10

Day 352

And you will be with him when time is over and no trace remains of dreams of spite in which you dance to death's thin melody.

D.U. ref.: 12. C90, *D.U.* page 392, *ACIM* location: C-6.5.6

CHAPTER 21

About the Disappearance of the Universe

Day 353

The images you make cannot prevail against what God Himself would have you be.

D.U. ref.: 1. T667, *D.U.* page 393, *ACIM* location: T-31.VIII.4

Day 354

There is no order of difficulty in miracles. One is not "harder" or "bigger" than another.

D.U. ref.: 2. T3, *D.U.* page 394, *ACIM* location: T-1.I.1

Day 355

Fairy tales can be pleasant or fearful, but no one calls them true. Children may believe them, and so, for a while, the tales are true for them. Yet when reality dawns, the fantasies are gone. Reality has not gone in the meanwhile.

D.U. ref.: 3. T170, *D.U.* page 397, *ACIM* location: T-9.IV.11.6

Day 356

You see the flesh or recognize the spirit. There is no compromise between the two. If one is real the other must be false, for what is real denies its opposite. There is no choice in vision but this one.

D.U. ref.: 4. T660, *D.U.* page 398, *ACIM* location: T-31.VI.1

Day 357

The lessons to be learned are only two. Each has its outcome in a different world. And each world follows surely from its source. The certain outcome of the lesson that God's Son is guilty is the world you see. It is a world of terror and despair.

D.U. ref.: 5. T646, *D.U.* page 398, *ACIM* location: T-31.I.7

Day 358

The Holy Spirit is the Translator of the laws of God to those who do not understand them. You could not do this yourself because a conflicted mind cannot be faithful to one meaning, and will therefore change the meaning to preserve the form.

D.U. ref.: 6. T115, *D.U.* page 398, *ACIM* location: T-7.II.4.5

Day 359

Perception's laws must be reversed, because they are reversals of the laws of truth.

D.U. ref.: 7. T554, *D.U.* page 400, *ACIM* location: T-26.VII.5.2

Day 360

Today I let Christ's vision look upon
All things for me and judge them not, but give
Each one a miracle of love instead.

D.U. ref.: 8. W478, *D.U.* page 400, *ACIM* location: W-349

Day 361

You will not remember change and shift in Heaven. You have need of contrast only here. Contrast and differences are necessary teaching aids, for by them you learn what to avoid and what to seek. When you have learned this, you will find the answer that makes the need for any differences disappear.

D.U. ref.: 9. T267, *D.U.* page 401, *ACIM* location: T-13.XI.6

Day 362

Guilt asks for punishment, and its request is granted. Not in truth, but in the world of shadows and illusions built on sin.

D.U. ref.: 10. T554, *D.U.* page 401, *ACIM* location: T-26.VII.3

Day 363

. . . And we are saved from all the wrath we thought belonged to God, and found it was a dream.

D.U. ref.: 11. W485, *D.U.* page 401, *ACIM* location: W.fl.in.5.3

Day 364

Salvation is undoing. If you choose to see the body, you behold a world of separation, unrelated things, and happenings that make no sense at all. This one appears and disappears in death; that one is doomed to suffering and loss. And no one is exactly as he was an instant previous, nor will he be the same as he is now an instant hence. Who could have trust where so much change is seen, for who is worthy if he be but dust? Salvation is undoing of all this. For constancy arises in the sight of those whose eyes salvation has released from looking at the cost of keeping guilt, because they chose to let it go instead.

D.U. ref.: 12. T660–661, *D.U.* page 407, *ACIM* location: T-31.VI.2

Day 365

I have forgotten no one. Help me now to lead you back to where the journey was begun, to make another choice with me.

D.U. ref.: 13. W330, *D.U.* page 407, *ACIM* location: W-rV.in.7.4

EPILOGUE

This book started with a short story, yet there is only one tale to tell. The eternally loved meet as one in God's womb. God has known us since before we found ourselves in this body, since ever. He knows us only within His own perfection and complete benevolence. Eternal gratitude is owed to God from the depths of our being, for always answering all of our prayers, and to our brother Jesus for hanging around until we all come home with Him.

In one of the many posts that I have sent to the *D.U.* online discussion board, I once took the liberty of formulating an *ACIM* inspired version of Psalm 23, which has also been one of my favorite prayers. I would like to share it with you as a gift. The words in **bold** come from *ACIM*-inspired thinking, and the equivalent words from the Psalm are *italicized* below each comparable idea.

God is my home. This world holds nothing that I want

> 1   *The LORD is my shepherd, I shall not be in want.*

The Peace of God is the answer to my every need, for I have only one need, and He has answered it,

> 2   *He makes me lie down in green pastures,*
> *he leads me beside quiet waters,*

He Creates me Whole, and then offers the Atonement when I turn away from His Love, and in Him I am eternally Whole and Holy

> 3   *he restores my soul.*

I walk with God in perfect Holiness. His Holiness is mine.

> *He guides me in paths of righteousness for his name's sake.*

Even though in my walk through this world, there may appear to be death,

> 4   *Even though I walk through the valley of the shadow of death,*

I will not buy into fear, I will see no evil, for I know You are in me

> *I will fear no evil, for you are with me;*

Your Love and your Word light up the way and guide and comfort me

> *your rod and your staff, they comfort me.*

I am at home in God dreaming of exile, and I am there with all my brothers as I have no enemies

> 5   *You prepare a table before me in the presence of my enemies.*

Your Love is eternally manifest in me; I am abundantly and forever Loved

> *You anoint my head with oil; my cup overflows.*

My happiness is guaranteed by God, as I awaken from this dream, I find my Self at Home with God Eternally Forever

> 6 *Surely goodness and love will follow me all the days of my life, and I will dwell in the house of the LORD forever.*

The love of God is always with us. May we learn to see, may we learn to hear His voice. May we learn to be the first to forgive, even if we're the only ones to do so at some point. May we learn to live *in* peace.

ACKNOWLEDGMENTS

Eternal thanks to Brad Langdon; Deborah Oakes; Jeane Weston; Patti Syrenka; my daughters Dianne and Alex for their contributions and help in editing and proofreading this book; and my son, Will, for his quiet wisdom.

I'm deeply grateful to Gary R. Renard for writing *D.U.* and sharing the all-inclusive and uncompromising message of God's love for His children in *A Course in Miracles* through the lens of his experience during those nine years. I'd also like to express my deep appreciation and eternal gratitude to the Foundation for A Course in Miracles and to Dr. Kenneth Wapnick for his tireless work and selfless giving so that the words of Jesus in *ACIM* reawaken our minds and help us return home to God.

About the Author

Martha Lucía Espinosa, who's originally from Colombia, is one of the most promising bilingual and bicultural authors in the area of inspirational and spiritual literature. At a young age, she moved to the United States and developed a very successful career in the information-technology field.

In addition to her professional success, Martha Lucía is known for her skillful and inspiring presentations and lectures on the principles of *A Course in Miracles (ACIM)* and translations of metaphysical and spiritual books and literature into and from Spanish and is a prolific and well-known contributor to various spiritual publications.

Her most recent work includes the translation of *The Disappearance of the Universe (D.U.)* by Gary R. Renard into Spanish, as well as the translation and Webmastering of his Website. She is also the lead moderator of, and a prolific contributor to, some of the fastest-growing online spiritual forums, one of which subscribes over 4,000 members, including readers of both *D.U.* and *ACIM*. For more information, please visit: **www.anotherwayfoundation.org.**

We hope you enjoyed this Hay House book. If you'd like to receive our online catalog featuring additional information on Hay House books and products, or if you'd like to find out more about the Hay Foundation, please contact:

Hay House, Inc., P.O. Box 5100, Carlsbad, CA 92018-5100
(760) 431-7695 or (800) 654-5126
(760) 431-6948 (fax) or (800) 650-5115 (fax)
www.hayhouse.com® • www.hayfoundation.org

———

Published in Australia by: Hay House Australia Pty. Ltd.,
18/36 Ralph St., Alexandria NSW 2015
Phone: 612-9669-4299 • *Fax:* 612-9669-4144
www.hayhouse.com.au

Published in the United Kingdom by: Hay House UK, Ltd.,
The Sixth Floor, Watson House, 54 Baker Street, London W1U 7BU
Phone: +44 (0)20 3927 7290 • *Fax:* +44 (0)20 3927 7291
www.hayhouse.co.uk

Published in India by: Hay House Publishers India,
Muskaan Complex, Plot No. 3, B-2, Vasant Kunj, New Delhi 110 070
Phone: 91-11-4176-1620 • *Fax:* 91-11-4176-1630
www.hayhouse.co.in

———

Access New Knowledge.
Anytime. Anywhere.

Learn and evolve at your own pace
with the world's leading experts.

www.hayhouseU.com

Printed in the United States
by Baker & Taylor Publisher Services